The Bipolar Guide to the Gift

Arlen Rundvall

Also by Arlen Rundvall
Fracture: A Memoir

Order this book online at www.trafford.com
or email orders@trafford.com

Most Trafford titles are also available at major online book retailers.

Note for Librarians: A cataloguing record for this book is available from Library
and Archives Canada at www.collectionscanada.ca/amicus/index-e.html

Printed in Victoria, BC, Canada.

ISBN: 978-1-4269-0426-4 (Soft)
ISBN: 978-1-4269-1106-4 (e-book)

*We at Trafford believe that it is the responsibility of us all, as both individuals
and corporations, to make choices that are environmentally and socially sound.
You, in turn, are supporting this responsible conduct each time you purchase a
Trafford book, or make use of our publishing services. To find out how you are
helping, please visit www.trafford.com/responsiblepublishing.html*

*Our mission is to efficiently provide the world's finest, most comprehensive
book publishing service, enabling every author to experience success.
To find out how to publish your book, your way, and have it available
worldwide, visit us online at www.trafford.com*

Trafford rev: 8/10/2009

 www.trafford.com

North America & international
toll-free: 1 888 232 4444 (USA & Canada)
phone: 250 383 6864 ♦ fax: 812 355 4082 ♦ email: info@trafford.com

Bipolar Reading Alert: Your reading ability and mind's retention may be affected by your condition: your medication and bipolar can hamper your ability to read. Take it easy, it can and will come back. Feel free to read this book in any order that you need to.

The life-changing results gained through the reading and following of the guidelines in this book will vary. The author and publisher take no responsibility for your positive or negative life changes. This book is intended to empower readers to make their own choices about their health. It is not designed to be a substitute for a professional health provider treatment plan. The writer and publisher are not responsible for any consequences or negative effects experienced by persons using this book. You, the individual will reap the good in your life. We are the responsible creators of our existence—embrace your power.

Thank you RosaLee: you give meaning to my life. Thanks for the encouragement.
Thank you to my family and friends for all your support and patience.
Thank you to the many health care professionals who assisted me throughout the years.
Thank you Alex Browne for the great editing!
Thank you Tracy D. Sim for the great photography!

This book is dedicated to the future generations of bipolar people. May it continue to become easier to live with and more of an opportunity.

Through balance flows the gift,
madness anoints my hands;
through ash I see the truth,
from sky, no limits bind.

Stay A.L.E.R.T.

Acknowledge that you are bipolar, and why.

Abstain from negative behaviors and substances.

Learn to recognize your thoughts, behaviors, and feelings to be up, down, psychotic, suicidal, or mixed states.

Liberate your thoughts, actions, and feelings toward positive.

Educate yourself—what works to ease you up or down or steady?

Edify your thoughts and actions.

Recognize what you need each moment to bring you up or down, and do it.

Review how what you do affects you and your mood.

Transport your wounded self back from traumatic events—feel.

Transform your future thoughts now—feel your dreams act real.

TABLE OF CONTENTS

"The possibility that each person is an infinite being is becoming more real now. Gifted with total flexibility in our nervous systems, we all have the choice to build boundaries or tear them down. Every person is continually manufacturing an infinite array of thoughts, memories, desires, objects, and so on. These impulses, rippling through the ocean of consciousness, become your reality. If you knew how to control the creation of impulses of intelligence, you would be able not only to grow new dendrites but anything else."
- Deepak Chopra, M.D.
Excerpt from his book, *Quantum Healing*

INTRODUCTION:

I strive in this book to take complete and integrated approaches to work through the negative illness traits of bipolar disorder; to plug into the gift side. Yes—there is a gift side. Even if you do not believe it now, you will in time know and appreciate what this so-called illness provides. Be open and you will be surprised. I hope that it takes you less time than my twenty years of suffering and learning.

Whether you are just diagnosed, or have spun your wheels for years, this book provides guidance. I have ridden my lunatic self to the ground and stepped off in a better place. You too can break through and surmount the odds. We are on a bipolar journey and to you I pass my baton of hope and vision.

There are many people in our society who have the positive touches of bipolar, and, few may know it. They are great with people and communicate to the heart. They create, paint, write, and sell. They are the bright lights. Some are not yet diagnosed, and others are diagnosed yet do not speak about bipolar to anyone.

This is not an academic or scientific book. I have scraped the trenches of bipolar and have had the good fortune to learn these many things to pass on to you.

This is your guide through mania, depression, psychosis, and mixed states. You can survive hospitalizations and hold your head up. You will get to the place where you know gratitude for the road you are on now: the ditch is dirty but worthy of growth. You can harness bipolar to serve you and yours. It can be a superpower touch. Hold on and learn—you can make bipolar your pinnacle of success.

At the end of each chapter—starting now—you'll find a list of springboards to thought and action.

Points of thought and action:
#1   Open my whole being to possibility.
#2   Open my mind to the ideas of this book.
#3   Do something good for myself.
#4   Listen to and identify a need of my mind and body for health.
#5   Meet this need of mine for health.
#6   (My personal plan.)

WELCOME TO THE FOLD

This blow of illness strikes deep in your flesh and soul—it has disrupted your life, your job, your education, your relationships, and your bank account. You may have gained weight from medication and lethargic behavior. You are out of touch with yourself; your appetite is altered, and your sleep is shot. You may have boozed and drugged yourself for remedy.

You are a disjointed fracture of head and heart. Perhaps you have spoken to your friends and family of your greatness and delusions of grandeur—how do you retract such statements? At one point, I believed I was to win the Nobel Prize and told a girlfriend this as fact.

You could be psychotic right now and not capable of comprehension. Sleep and eat and walk, be gentle to yourself: you will come back. Give it time, take your medication. Every psychosis is different but the breaks from reality all share this—we psychotics leave the reality walkers behind. I was changed and my friends and family remained the same. They do not know this part of me, and never fully will. Some can be compassionate and open to my wounds. Others cannot even have a conversation about bipolar.

It is something that naturally repels people—it is even hard to accept yourself in these experiences. It takes time. You are not the only one who has experienced what you are going through: it will surprise you to meet people who have experienced the very same details as your madness.

I remember talking to a fellow manic psychotic a few years after my first episode. I told him of my psychotic time traveling to the Garden of Eden, and the testing to return to the present day. He experienced the

1

same themes of psychosis—it was a revelation to me. I AM NOT THE ONLY ONE. You are not the only one to experience this madness, either.

We can have related themes of psychosis because we are exposed to the same world. Our minds distort similar information, and it just makes sense that we could share similar trips.

We are a loose tribe of torn souls. We have been presented with a gauntlet of opportunity. Insanity opens your person to new vistas of thoughts and abilities. I am a changed person for being psychotic several times; now I am thankful and would not change these episodes.

Margot Kidder mentioned in *Beyond Crazy: Journeys Through Mental Illness* (reference #1) that, for her healing, she had to accept the fact that these delusions and intricacies of psychosis actually happened. They were reality for her. I agree. In my case I, too, had to accept these weird scary situations of mind creation as reality. I could not keep them separate from me. Bizarre stuff happened. It was real, I allowed myself to feel the emotion of those events: I cried and healed.

When I was psychotic, I did not feel any usual emotion; I knew at times I should feel a certain way but had no experience or release of the emotion. A backlog of unfelt events built up in my system and contributed to my illness. I had to embrace these realities and process them with my full being—creating a picture or music or even a sculpture out of mashed potatoes can help in processing these crazy realities. Creating something, anything, can help you in this progression.

Our experiences can be far removed from society and it is logical that we can bring something new back to society—we can create souvenirs influenced by our journeys. In doing this, you will create a bridge for your mind to be in society. People will not understand, usually, the experience but they most likely will appreciate your unique creation. And with creative refinement, they will appreciate your innovations even more.

I don't understand everything that happened. Maybe I will some day, and that's all right. But I embraced the things I did and my pride grieved the shameful acts while I accepted my little psychotic creature. It all added up to help. The creature no longer comes out to play very often.

I hated to become a good actor, but that is part of the training to master the polarities of bi. We have to present a different front from our true internal lives. I believe many people can't handle the truth.

There is substance to the expression, "Fake it till you make it." You can act yourself out of corners of mood. You will make yourself engage in activities and with people and have to act, totally, to get through, but the experience of social and action will react in your brain to move you toward health in the smallest way. Eventually it will be less like acting and more real, you will be making your steps toward health.

What goes up must come down. It intrigues me how different the symptoms of depression can be. For me, I slept as much as possible—my only pleasure was dreaming another reality. To operate your being in front of you—like a dead meat puppet—is a gray place.

Depression is a lonely perverse blanket. I miss it—doesn't that sound twisted? But it was a strange ego friend, warped in love. I chose not to go there but it took many years to counter the place. I still have quick leanings but I get kicked out fast. I eat, sleep, exercise, and change my thinking—easier said than done, I'll admit.

I changed the intensity and duration of my depression by living my life differently. I faced my life and fears and lived so I would not have any regrets. This takes lifelong practice. What a wonderful thing at ninety years of age to think back and smile—you faced it all and have no regrets. Sounds good to me. I started living my life the way I needed to, not for other people or to screw people over, but to be true to my self and who I needed to be.

The greatest preventative for me against deep depression is to prevent and reduce my manic highs and psychosis. For years I struggled in futility to prevent the high fractures. My doctor at the time did not help me prevent my yearly cycle. He would also overmedicate me. I believe this overmedication contributed, to slingshot me into depression. It is a grand combination of forces and events that can affect us.

Our purpose in this book is to be empowered to be self-aware—to master the evil that bipolar can be. We have to be mean and ruthless at times, yet we also need to pamper and baby ourselves.

In the depths of depression we need to celebrate anything—in that desert place of nothing we must take minute steps toward the oasis. I would get to a spot where I could not do one thing all day or night. I lay, numbed, in bed. I kicked myself to shower and enjoyed it on some level and celebrated the achievement and perhaps I could do another thing, it did not matter what. I did shower and it was great. Maybe tomorrow I could go for a walk. I would go back to bed; eventually I would do something else.

Your road to recovery can be quicker with the help of this book. Ultimately, because we are all different, you need to amend this book to suit your mind and body to come up with unique techniques that will help you alone. Some of the things in this book may seem strange but they worked for me. Rather than judging me, discover what you need to do to live healthier.

If you have generational problems, leave them with your parents: they did not receive the grace to deal with what their parents gave them. But you do have the grace, mercy, and tenacity to let their negative tendencies go. You can and will deal with it: whether it be abuse or alcoholism, it doesn't matter what. You have the power to deal with the generational curses. You can find the patterns of your mother and father, and destroy the lattice of deceit.

Bipolar has a generational aspect. Perhaps we need to look at it as a lineage of gifting. Sometimes it takes generations to harness the creature of gift. It can be a monster but let's not call the creature a monster—then it will always be a monster. A creature can go both ways. I for one am mastering this creature for good.

I hope that this book will assist you in your personal journey to freedom, so that you, too, can say you would not choose another. I believe I have the best illness in the world. This is not a sick thing to say. I love who I am and what this illness has created in me. It has knocked down the walls I had built. It has made me a different person with unique challenges.

I still dislike my tendency to be over-stimulated—I take in too many details of personal interaction. I then have to unwind my mind to sleep. If I get over tired then I am more sensitive. I view these challenges as fine-tuning. I learn to distance myself from certain situations, and to guard my sleep further.

We experience unique occurrences; but I hope we may meet together in these pages. I strive for honesty in this book. Through my transparency, may you find the hope, courage and drive to counter the creature into a manageable corner. It may just present you with brightly wrapped packages. You will give thanks. You will be changed into a better person. I believe it is the greatest opportunity in this world. We have to look at it this way.

Embrace your messed-up self—you can do it, one step at a time. It may take years and there will be many opportunities for review—you will have to face the same things over and over. Get a great attitude and plow right through these large problems in your life. It is great when they become automatic to deal with.

We will talk about sex, food, exercise, personal relations, your doctor, your tool kit, spirituality, giving up your highs, giving up your lows, moving on, stigma, medication, psychosis, self-medicating, money, and many more themes of bipolar and your bettering.

We will get to the place where we need less medication (SLOWLY with doctor's assistance.) We will become free of entering the hospital—this was a huge step for me. I thought I would be in one every winter for the rest of my life. I came to realize that there was an undertone by certain doctors that encouraged this interdependence. It took me close to a decade of practice to free myself. It was a tough journey. Now I've experienced a decade of freedom from hospitalizations. And then I spent three nights in a psychiatric center—but it was a quick recovery.

It was great for me to be hospitalized at certain times. Lately I have been missing aspects of those hospitalizations—the excitement edge and the camaraderie. Those smoking and lounge rooms were where I most communed with people. We shared and danced the sharp fringes of lunacy and the outlands wore us to be brothers and sisters without shame or judgment for the odd behavior that drove us.

May we commune in this book and celebrate the common template that is thrown like a thick blanket over us. We bipolar people have similarities—it intrigues me how close certain experiences are. I would love to hear back from you concerning your journey and how this book has helped you to reduce illness and find the positive (www. thebipolarguide.com).

I promise great things in this book because this is a great illness. We have the comic book ability to enhance our introvert into extrovert. But all the while there is a danger we could fall into the statistical realm of suicide. We absolutely need to take this illness seriously. We need to dwell around the equator of mood—you have the power of the poles, but know the dangers: leave the ice and perilous seas to the penguins and join the party in the sun.

The world is ready for you, another actualized bipolar. I do not want to feed your ego and delusions of grandeur if you are having any—this is something we all have to work through; but you do have special abilities that only you can have. And remember that no matter how big you are in the world, just like any queen or president or rock star, you are still just a person with human needs.

You are a human being in spite of where you have been and what you have thought and acted upon. We need to make the best of it and choose to enjoy our life. No one else will.

Points of thought and action:
#1   I am not the only one to experience this madness—I am not a freak.
#2   Accept all the craziness that I've been through as my reality and feel and mourn those experiences and hurt. (I am careful to not overdo this, and proceed at a healthy rate.)
#3   Who am I? How has bipolar changed me?
#4   Dream of a life with bipolar positives.
#5   Trust my creative urge and follow it through to create something.
#6   (My personal plan.)

ATTITUDE—THE OPPORTUNITY

Happiness is a decision and a chosen state to journey in. Have you decided to be happy? Joy is joy, in spite of circumstances. It is a power to not be affected by every little thing that goes wrong. Stretch your ways of thinking. There are many purposes behind what goes on; we don't always know why, or need to know, for that matter.

If you tend to be like me and be over analytical at times, you have to slow your brain down and let things go. We don't have to figure everything out. Study nature—a great aspect is how it rolls with the storms. Trees bend in the wind. If you can't bend with the wind you may end with your roots pulled up. You might end up in the hospital.

A great bipolar challenge for me has been the enhanced awareness and active mind. I get stimulated easily in social situations. I take in more details than I used to. In the early stages of mania I would involve myself in strangers' conversations. I had bridges to the world and the openness to pursue them. I meet someone and for that person it is a small encounter. For me, I take in the background and other conversations and why things are the way they are. My mind wants to process the entire situation.

It is great as a writer but it can be automatic and impossible to shut off. I can find it difficult to focus on the conversation I am in—any words spoken within my hearing tend to have to be processed. It can be great fun to observe and learn and it can be hard not to be rude to my friend. It helps to be in a quieter place. And it all depends on my mood and amount of sleep.

Mania can supply an incredible attitude: you are open and free to other people, you are invincible, yet you have no ego. You are capable

of anything, you think big and act big, not out of ego but because of
the reality of zero limitations. Living with this illness has blown open
my doors of possibility. It has given me confidence to pursue anything
my heart desires. I wrote three screenplays and traveled to a California
pitchfest; I pitched my stories to producers. Two of the screenplays are
being read. If bipolar was not in my life I don't think this would have
happened.

If I can stay tuned to a bit of the possibility and excitement of manic
life, outside mania, I will be a better person. My relationships will be
alive and my life will be worth living. I will be moving forward and
not standing still. I believe if you stand still, your surroundings and
experience will slide you backwards. You have to fight to better your
existence. You cannot wait for this illness to have its way with you: it
will consume with a vengeance.

We need to rise up with fight to face our day, whether it is in
hospital, disappointment or extreme mood. This illness plays out in our
head: it is an internal war that is waged. Stats for bipolar suicide are
high—why do you think so many of us do it?

It can be a lonely driven place. I found insanity to be a foe that had
no kindness, no peace, no comfort, no love, and no joy. I struggled for
years with the negative side of this thing. It rode me hard. I did not
know if I would make it or die.

It is hard to face your fallen life. You've been fired or had to quit
another job or school. You have to face your classmates or friends as a
mentally ill person. People are alienated by the experience: we find out
about true friendship.

For some control type people it is hard to be with someone who
has lost control of their situation. I think this is a valid generalization:
people who are free to relax and go with the flow are better able to relate
to a bipolar, it is easier for them to be friends; and for others, it can be
their personality that sets them up to never be able to associate with
a bipolar. It is their previous issues that repel them from you. We can
only change ourselves.

The greatest advantage in facing any great problem is the belief that
a solution will present itself. I believed, like Edison, that I could find
a solution. He kept trying filaments to get the right one for the light
bulb. When an approach failed, he was happy that he had eliminated
something that couldn't work.

At times, I felt like I was making no progress as I struggled year after year in improving my situation with the illness. It was horrible. I despised what this illness did to my relationships. Strain is a weak word for it. I felt I would never regain a stable and happy existence. I tried everything and discovered things that did not help me—medications and lifestyle changes that made no effect. But all the while I was building a small case of approaches that worked. It took time to learn about the illness and my self.

Hope was my greatest ally. There were a few dark times when I lost sight of it—dangerous. For many reasons, I was able to always maintain and regain hope to face the next day: a new day with which to try to make it a little better. That is the gauntlet when you are facing suicide in a corner by yourself.

How do we get out of those situations? By crawling to borrow someone else's hope. And for me, I believe, by the grace of God. Why? Maybe so I could write this book.

I believe many factors came together to remedy my situations. My brutal honesty was a great tool. I would still be a mess if I couldn't have been honest with my addictive tendencies. Honesty also helped in dealing with my doctor. My support networks have worked on honesty alone. When I recruited someone in an official role on my support team, and we agreed on something for me to work on, I had to be honest. It was the only way. Who are we kidding by deceiving in this life?

Bipolar is enough of a challenge; we do not need bad attitudes to complicate things. Outlook is huge. How do you face a situation? Optimism is a massive power. In writing this book I have been made aware of the word illness. But I don't like using the word illness in describing bipolar: then it will always be an illness. I have been there and burned the t-shirt. Please do not refer to my bipolar aspect as an illness. We have no need for those that would keep us down and sick.

To get a life, I have had to develop a new approach to my situation. I have changed to look at bipolar as an opportunity and it has become that and more. It is a large door I have passed through and everything is different and new. My life will never be the same. It is an exciting adventure full of life and pleasure, and challenge.

I dwelled in a long dark tunnel for many years; I could feel myself, over a couple of years, approach the end of the tunnel and fall out into the great world that I live in now. How do you get through your dark tunnel? For each of us it is different. What helps you get through another day and limit suffering?

A sense of humor is vital. I have had to laugh at myself when I ran out of tears. I could only cry so much. I had to grieve the loss of my youth. This bipolar stole my twenties from me—that is one way of looking at it. If I had kept a bad attitude, it would have been my thirties and forties too. I would have been dead.

We need to choose our battles and let the rest go—certain things are not worth concerning ourselves with. I still have not mastered driving and being endangered by other drivers—when they cut in too close in front of me. Usually I can let it go, but occasionally it still pisses me off. We all have our triggers and it is our responsibility to be aware of them and choose to be affected or not.

Does it really matter ten years from now or even one week from now if someone cuts me off? No. Then I won't let it steal even five minutes of my good chosen attitude and mood. I work hard to focus on good emotions and live to maintain them, I have to guard them and not get set off by things that do not matter. Power over you is only power when you allow it to be.

We live in a busy challenging world. We are losing our niceness; it is becoming a cooler, impersonal world. Can you choose to keep your good attitude in spite of what goes on around you? It can be the biggest challenge, but it also provides the largest paybacks. The same event happens to two different people and their reactions are opposite. Their inner world colors their response—their past experiences and their attitudes press their emotional triggers.

You can train your mind to process a situation and decide to react differently. You can choose to let a situation go and move on, to not let it affect you for the next hour. You could get into a bad attitude, then you take that approach with you to your next encounters and attract more of the same. If you don't give your head a shake you could be in this negative state your whole day and the next.

It is our choice to be happy. How will you choose? You have bipolar: it can be horrible. You have had to suspend your education—will you slip into suicide? It happens, but not to you; you have to decide your reality. This can be a serious condition that can take you for horrible rides. You have to fight back with good attitude.

Sure you have to grieve for getting it. Bipolar can screw up every aspect of your known existence: your family may abandon you or you may alienate yourself. Your spouse may divorce you, you may lose your job, your career, your friends, your house, and your chosen place to live. You might gain a hundred pounds and have medication temporarily steal your ability to think or read. You are in a suicidal depression—all you think about is how to kill yourself and you are starting to not care about the mess you would leave for others to clean up.

Hello, I got out of that rut and you can too, I cleaned up my mess and am building a new life. It turns out to be a blessing to not be able to chase after life the way everyone else was. I am a better person for my derailment. I know who I am and what I value. I have priorities and don't waste my time on things that do not matter.

The superficial has burned away. It makes it hard for me to be superficial with people. I can do it for a while but it is a waste of time. Life is short. If you need to be a shallow, unhappy person that is okay, I can walk away and come back later and see if you have changed. We all change for the better or worse. When I come back and see people again, I notice the difference in them. You have to keep moving forward to make progress. It is my life and I don't have to spend time with people who bring me down or cannot accept who I am.

It can be a hard thing to grow out of your friends or family. You love them and would like to see them live their life fully in joy, but just like nobody can do it for you, we cannot live for other people. I try to live my life as an example and move on to where I feel I need to be. I have things I want to see and do. I want to help people and make a difference. I want to give back. I have to leave certain people in the past. Maybe my loved ones will watch me and be inspired to make their own changes in mind and situation.

Sometimes when we choose to live a certain way, people cannot accept our new lives and they try to bring us down. People we love can be the hardest on us. Sometimes it can be because they are afraid to change themselves. Change is scary—it seems easier to accept things the way they are.

The world around you changes with or without you. You can be left in an unhappy place, or you can adapt to where you need to be. We all have different hang-ups from our upbringing. Which of your potential hang-ups do you want to keep and which do you need to walk away from?

A relatively short time ago our life expectancy was thirty years of age. Perhaps we have not adjusted to this yet and many of us have trouble improving our life enjoyment. It is no longer for many just about food and shelter. Too many choices can paralyze. Perhaps as bipolar, we have an advantage to adapt in the world and improve our places of attitude and situation—bipolar has shaken our world to the very core of self. There were many times I had no clue as to who I was and where I was. I was hammered to nothing, but I rose again to reclaim a life. I was struck down and climbed back up to stand.

Everything in my life was obliterated and I chose to find and cultivate a great attitude and here I am: I love my wife, my home, where I live, and what I do for money and recreation. I create books and make money—how great is that? And it provides therapy. I love life and it is not long enough for my taste.

When I did get my problems sorted out, the many traits for surviving and regaining my sanity worked to produce momentum: my life quickly came together for good. I was accustomed to adapting to major changes and rolling with the punches and getting back up to smile.

This book is one hundred percent on the attitude of self-responsibility. This is the key for the whole approach to the gift: you have to develop your attitude to see possibility and potential in this bipolar. You have to move on from looking at it as an illness. You have nothing to lose. You can only move forward. Look out world; we have another bipolar waking up to his or her potential.

I am sorry, but I feel bad for many people who are not bipolar; they coast through their life to a place of mundane. Gray is a great place if you want it, but many people hate their lives and cannot do anything about it. Bipolar forced me to the very bone to face death down and to choose life. It taught me to take risks and to live in balance to survive.

With all great approaches to illness we see common threads. We have to go through the stages of grieving over aspects of our life. We then have to rally the troops and make the best of it. Simply staying alive—whatever it takes—can be a huge accomplishment with bipolar. If you are alive today you are a hero. If you are reading or listening to this I am very impressed. You are capable of comprehension, and on your way.

We are forced to face our values, what we think is important in life. I need to live close to nature. I need to be in good relation with people. I need to create to feel best: it acts like a pressure relief valve for me.

What is in this bipolar that is opportunity? It knocked the socks off my introvert tendencies. I still prefer to have my corner of the room leanings, yet mania has developed social skills. I can work the crowd and bridge to people. I can surge with confidence to set people at ease. I can be diplomatic.

I have used the increased thinking of bipolar to my advantage. I love to learn and discover more of this world I live in. It is great to have an active mind. Life is short and I absorb more and live deeper.

I have experienced the heights and the depths of mood: what a challenge that is. Talk about tourism. Tough to get through with your life, but hey, who does in the end? That was a joke. We will all die someday, hopefully after a good life. That is the point of attitude. The same events can tear your heart open or be laughed at, depending on your perception.

Attitude is more important than any medication. I have seen much medication thrown at people who have a sick-thinking attitude. It falls on sour ground. It helps them to a certain point and they fall back into their hole. With great attitude you can use less medication and it will prosper within you to heal.

Your whole life will smooth out. We cannot have the 'poor me' attitude; sure your life is terrible; yes, I care, but get over it. The sooner you move on, the quicker you will create and embrace the good in your life.

If you keep focusing on the past negative, you will keep moving in that direction. We need to turn around and head away from the negative in our lives. Hang around a shit-pile long enough and it will be hard to get the stink off. Walk away and start thinking in new ways of possibility. If you can think of new great ways for your life, you can live it. It may take time but go for it.

I want to be fertile ground. Sure plenty of weeds grow but I get my exercise by pulling them. Enough flowers and fruit will grow too.

Study attitude; listen to music that makes you feel good. Watch TV and movies that encourage you to live a richer life. Expose yourself to less advertising and it will help you be content with what you have.

Read things that encourage you. Life is short. Do the things you need to do.

We live in a time when we can choose unique paths more than ever before. The variety of pursuits you can follow to earn money is astounding. Our grandparents had fewer choices. This is a small factor in our generational gaps. Previous generations have little comprehension of growing up in today's world. I have little understanding, yet am aware of the differences. But this wide-open world can bring more confusion and stress to our decision making.

In certain ways it is harder to live in a place with too many choices. I over analyze things. Sometimes it is better for me to shop in a store with fewer choices: I have to cross compare and it takes too much time and energy to select between thirty different toilet paper packages. Give me three choices and I'll be able to make the choice quicker and with less energy. Ours is a smaller world, with more access, but much more complicated than ever before.

We mix all the religions into a pot now—we are no longer separated by geography. We are exposed to more cultures and ways of life. We are bombarded with media information and advertisements. We always have to buy to be happy. "It is the only way," these commercials tell us. The carrot is always out of our reach. Does it help me to hear about wars and murders and fires across the country? We focus on the negative—perhaps that is partially why our world seems to worsen: we manifest more of what we focus on.

I have to limit my exposure to the negative—and all information. I need time to process and placate the outside turbulence within me. I have to regurgitate it out sometimes in writing—it makes me feel at peace and I can live more engaged in the world. I can't read certain newspapers because they only have negative headline stories: tell me something good about the world.

That is partially why I like to, and need to, hang out in nature. It does not fill my head with evil deeds and corporate greed. The worst I will see is how our progress is destroying nature. That, too, I find hard to take but I planted a tree last week. I feel good about that. I consume less than I want to. I say no to myself.

I am a bad citizen for our Gross National Product. I would like to improve my health and happiness and live in community more than drive profits up for shareholders and CEO's. I would rather spend time getting to know you than just consuming more stuff.

My great attitude cultivation needs a forest to walk in and breathe deeply. One of the reasons I chose not to have kids was that I could not foresee explaining the world to them. We are a selfish bunch of people. Could we make our world a better place for our kids before having them? Where are your priorities? Maybe I just think too much. And isn't the world a better place?

I am responsible and choose to make this illness into a gift; not be a burden to others, but to enhance the lives of those around me. I want to leave the world a happier, healthier place. I am selfish. I like gifts. I am definitely going to open up this bipolar to the point of gift-hood. Are you? It is your choice. With or without you the world happens. How can you live your best in it?

I try to live in peace and joy with my enhanced bipolar. It has given me an increased awareness and exposure to suffering in the world. My times in psychiatric wards showed me that life is tainted with suffering and angst. And in the midst of suffering one can construct an island of refuge, and build on it new ways of thinking and acting.

Points of thought and action:
#1   In what present attitude do I face bipolar?
#2   What attitude do I need to face bipolar?
#3   I believe in solutions to my problems.
#4   How can I train my mind to react better to situations?
#5   How is my honesty and sense of humor?
#6   (My personal plan.)

DIAGNOSIS

Was your first reaction to being labeled bipolar, shock and denial? Were you pissed off and angry? It is normal to feel a variety of responses to the news that you have a mental illness. In our beginning times of illness we most often find ourselves in medical care. Usually we receive the diagnosis in the midst of crises—we are in the depths of despair and or psychotic and are not in our ideal state to deal with stress. Receiving the news of a major mental illness ranks up there on the stress charts. Even at your optimum normal you would be shook up to get the call that you have bipolar.

It is good to react to the news—it is bad news: cry, grieve, and scream. If it is a proper diagnosis, your old personality is somewhat gone and you will be forever different. To begin with, all could be terrible and bad. Just go with it—try to feel and embrace the experience.

Talk to people. You will learn who your friends are and who will leave you—let them go. This is part of the package: you get to know who your true friends are. Bipolar will repel people who cannot handle the new truths of your life—they will be the ones missing out in the long run. You will make new and deeper friends.

Throw a party with your friends to mourn your old person and to celebrate your newness of personality—this is a gift that has chosen you. If you can do this you are advanced and will run through and into the gift stages with speed.

Or you may be like me, a 'cry-on-your-own-in-the-bathtub' type of person. Light a candle—you will need help to find your way through the mires of illness to your gift. We each need to react differently to the news that we are bipolar: unique approaches to deal with and process the information. Denial, anger, fear, remorse, self-pity, blame, and hatred are a few of your options.

Your doctor is there to help you. Use him or her for your best treatment. A doctor is just one of many professionals on your team. They may counsel you and or focus on your drug plan of treatment. It is vital to work with them.

This illness has built in rebellions against doctors, and help via medications. You might feel compelled to walk into the wilderness to heal—it is all you can do to resist. I would encourage you to work with your doctor first and do your fine-tuning later in the wilderness. Your deluded self may tell you that shots of whiskey are better for you than medication. I was not always able to resist the urges, I made progress and later learned which urges were good and to be followed and this changed as time went on.

If you ever wanted a challenge in life, you have it now.

There is a place for being psychotic or suicidal and depressed. The psychiatric ward has been my safe harbor many times. It has protected me from my own suicidal hands and provided walls for my psychotic self to run into and begin to reform into human self. There are few other places that can handle us in our extremes. Retreat centers, hotels, and relatives may have certain benefits but be careful of your symptoms and the severity.

Especially in the beginning, you absolutely need to take this seriously—your life and the lives of your loved ones depend on it. Trust your doctors and nurses and professionals.

Chances are your doctor may have trouble in this arena of diagnoses. It can take a few tries. One encounter is not enough to see the up and the down. And they don't usually see us when we are so-called normal, to have a comparative point of reference.

Bipolar has many recipes—some of us are more up than down. Others are more down than up. Some of us have a regular calendar connection. I was a more predictable cycle—hooked up to the calendar year. But it took time to recognize the pattern.

My favorite early diagnosis was, "Hyperactive manic-depressive with overtones of schizophrenia." It was hard to live up to! Earlier I had self-medicated myself into a street drug-induced psychosis. I gained sanity back and was fine for a couple years. Then I fell into a large crack of psychosis. It took a while to get spit out. The doctor diagnosed me as schizophrenic. He had only seen me this one hospitalization, yet needed to label me.

I remember feeling devastated—my sister brought me a clipping on the illness and I cried and screamed out the vehicle window. What a horrible pronouncement—was it a prophecy? It said I would not have meaningful work or a significant other, and I would have a tough life. I mean no offense to our schizophrenic friends. Do we not know there are exceptions within every category? Why are we so quick to categorize?

Even if I had schizophrenia, why do people need to limit me? It will be disappointing regardless—you can still prepare me for changes but change the wording: it will be a challenge to have meaningful work, a significant other...

A few years later I experienced several psychotic breaks and was informed I would be on major tranquilizers for life. Hello in there, who are you to hinder my dreams and ideals? The way it was communicated to me was certain—there was no escape from such pharmaceutical need.

Please: if you have just been diagnosed as mentally ill, take it easy on yourself. It is not the end of the world. Do not focus on the "You won't be able to do this, or that." You can do anything you want. Give yourself time and believe.

We as people like to keep others down where we are, or in a predictable place. The world would be a brighter place if every mentally ill person got his or her life together and moved from dependency to independence. I believe we would have solutions to many of our problems. We would have more beautiful art, music, and books. Engineering solutions would abound. We would have deeper relationships with our families and neighbors and not watch reality TV. We would be living reality, our reality of choice.

Doctors are there to assist you. Be open to their ways of helping you. When we get to a certain point of suffering, whether it is up or down, pharmaceuticals are the best way to help. They used to put us in cages, all over the world. These pills and injections are our friends. We must learn to co-operate and communicate with our doctors to our best recovery.

I have had a spectrum of doctors—from gifted saint to ego-driven enabler. There are great healers in their midst and there are people in it primarily for the money and power. They are human like the rest of us: we all run the spectrum from saint to scum.

The key thing to remember about doctors is they hold the goods—pharmaceuticals are the major building blocks that help us and keep us stable. Lifestyle choices and discipline are the minor tunings; though guarding sleep and exercising can help prevent a high. These drugs fast track our journey to health. But for doctors and their medicines, I would not be alive today. They saved my life several times.

In time your lifestyle choices may have a bigger impact on your life than medications. But when the symptoms loom large, pharmaceuticals assist to the greatest degree.

Your doctor is one of your many lifelines. It is your responsibility to fix yourself. One pill will usually not do it. You may be fortunate that the first drug you try is the one designed for you—it brings you down or up or keeps you stable. Give thanks and live your life well.

Chances are you will have some troubles with your medications and side effects. This is part of the price—the drugs are improving each decade. Remember the cages of centuries ago: we live in a grand time to be mentally ill, and it is getting better. Hang in there, and communicate with your doctor concerning your side effects and problems. Maybe you are on too much tranquilizer and can't even walk.

If you sit around all day, it makes sense that you won't sleep well and that you need more medication to sleep. Our bodies were made for movement; that is when we operate and feel best.

We have not evolved into our sedate systems yet. I don't think we will without more medicalization. We need to counter with treatments for heart disease and diabetes. Our systems are not adapting fast enough to counter our sedate lifestyles.

Educate yourself—your life depends on it. Yes, I care what good professionals think about my health, but they don't really know me and what I am capable of, what I know. Who knows what goes on in your head but you?

You are in there every day of your life if you are healthy—many people in our society escape from the mirror and the pillow. Are you self-medicating with booze or drugs? Are you with the right significant other? Are you over your parents' and siblings' influence?

You have to be fully in your head to make the best of bipolar. It is a tough road ahead, yet you have your whole life. In case you are trying geographical escapes, it will follow you to the ends of the earth.

This book is intended for bipolar people. We used to be called manic-depressives. I prefer the term bipolar, it is more mysterious and baffling to people. If they ask, I get to inform them first of the high part, the mania. I found in the old days that people heard only depressive in the phrase, manic-depressive, and then they shut their ears. I grew tired of people only partly understanding the down part. They seemed to be afraid of the manic side. People are smart.

We can be too big for our situation—it is hard to fit in, but we can. You've journeyed through rough places to get to where you are: it will be a tough harrowing trip to ride this illness down and to harness it to your gift. But I believe it's within you, waiting to come out.

Perhaps you are in the hospital for the first time. It can be a wild place to dwell: hard to believe sometimes that it is intended for our good. I always found that when I was hospitalized I deteriorated before I improved. I am a sensitive person in regard to others. I can connect in a quick, deep manner. But it can be a bad trait when you live in close proximity to thirty mentally ill people—I would enter their dramatics and emotional angst. I would become them: their feelings would shake me up. All this occurred when I needed fewer stimuli and more rest. I struggled for years to gain some independence and check into a hotel to lower stimulus, instead of running into the psychiatric ward.

The most important aspect of diagnoses is for you to kick yourself to self-knowledge—is it true that you are bipolar? You live in your head full time. It is not worth it to live in denial. Do your own education on what you face. We are blessed to live in this time. Yet there are still places on earth that persecute the mentally ill.

You must get it in your head that you are your own best friend. You have to design your situation to suit you. You have to come to grips with your diagnoses. It took me several years to sort through my drug and alcohol use. Was I just self-medicating the illness? I still do not know for certain. It seems like I was an addict for a while but, for years now, I am not a drug addict, I am bipolar. Sometimes we will never know why certain things are the way they are.

Perform your homework. Write notes to yourself. Keep a health journal. Track your days on a chart—make a number system: the number one could represent suicidal thinking, two could represent whatever your depths of depression are. Mine meant disappearing into my bed and sleep. Make your own chart and personalize it. I believe you are more creative than you realize. Have fun in designing your own charting system. It can be a vital step in your beginning road. Five could represent your normal equatorial self: your moods flow freely and do not control you.

Perhaps you need a couple of symbols to represent the type and degree of mixed states. I hated this rapid cycling and I found it to be a scary ride. Perhaps use a star symbol to represent major ups and downs within an hour. A circle could be used to represent major ups and downs within a twenty-four hour period. The $ sign could represent a manic spending tendency. (^) could be delusions of grandeur. < = > could be hypersexual. Have some fun with it, make it your own. There are templates available in books and online.

(About mixed states: please note) this is a dangerous place to be! Watch yourself. Kay Redfield Jamison writes in *Night Falls Fast: Understanding Suicide* (reference #2) that mixed states are the most dangerous for suicide attempts and their success. You have the depth of depression and suicidal ideals and lack proper thinking; combine all this with a mood swing up to energy and action, and you may have stumbled onto your recipe to be a suicide statistic.

My one carried-out suicide attack took place in one of these mixed states. I was in my only drug-induced psychosis; I had the depressive delusion that I was responsible for the destruction of the world and I had the energy rush to do something to atone for that delusion. I survived the gory details to write about it in *Fracture: A Memoir.*

This is an illness that can kill you and we need a serious approach to survive. To doctors we are a patient—it is not life or death for them. We may be blessed to have a good doctor. My greatest doctor still stands out to me as my savior: he gave me the keys to my freedom. After many years and several doctors, it all came together in perfect timing.

The number seven on your chart could be that place where you are optimized human. I would like to patent and bottle that place. We could be rich beyond this sphere. Have you lived in this place where everything works better, where you think and talk smoother? Your senses are heightened. Sight, smell, taste, sex, and everything is incredible. I found it to be better than cocaine, and no, I don't want you to do cocaine. I happened to do cocaine and years later experienced hypo and I would choose the hypo every time. It is natural, that is what amazed me. This is part of who I am, this wild comic-book enhancement of all that is good.

I have met people who have lived predominately at this stage for many years—they can have the tendency to wear their bodies down and out. For me this fast place used to lead to higher numbers. My number eight would include loss of sleep and a slip out of touch with reality. Nine would see me with delusions of grandeur and following my psychotic creature commands. This level would usually include spiritual tangents of delusion.

I found that if I lost sleep in the hypo stage, I would tend to gain momentum and the ride would take me. I would lose touch and soar toward the heavens. If only you could journey to those places and be sane immediately. It usually took me seven to eight months after the psychotic break to start feeling solid in my true self again.

My ten required the intervention of others. I needed help to regain life. I recommend to you that you have a place, when up or down, where you consult your doctor automatically. If I hit an eight or a two I will talk to my doctor. Decide when to do it before you get to the point: the decision will be automatic and brilliant in hindsight. You will prevent deeper suffering.

The point of all this tracking is to be more aware of who you are in bipolar. You can use this as a tool to approach your doctor to secure different medications for different times of the year, to reduce your medications at certain times. We are complex beings that are difficult to trace, the origins of our triggers are complex and hard to nail down. This system will help you realize your lifestyle choices and how they affect you.

It does no good for a psychiatrist to diagnose you with something if you deny it. The illness will cover you in its horror. You can deny it to your grave—have a good time with that.

This is your life. Who are you? Is the diagnosis true? Is it a little off? Without tracking yourself, you can lose touch with your world of existence. Bipolar can steal your self-awareness. It can take a long time to get a good observational handle on your life of bipolar. The quicker you start charting, the quicker you can remedy the situation.

Sure you can enjoy aspects of the illness uncontrolled—but it bites back. I met a man who entered and opened his hyper sexuality side of mania. He wrote a book about it. Good time—to sleep with hundreds of people! When is it enough? He killed himself.

We have a grim outcome if we frolic in the outreaches of this illness. I hated my first years of the illness. It was human shock—a culture shock that included psychotic episodes and the distance of stigma, a good time to have your family stay away from you. An insane person is hard to be around. We can be fun, but we're usually just draining and scary. Most healthy people are not accustomed to unpredictable actions and words: we like our relationships to be predictable.

Have you pained enough? Do you believe that you are bipolar? Ask the doctor and nurses questions. They have seen and know much about the illness. Use all your resource people. Some can be biased, therefore spread your platform of knowledge so it can stand on its own. Read books if you can. I was not able to read when I was manic or extremely depressed or on certain medications. Get someone else to read for you.

Take your time and be easy on yourself. There may be certain months or entire years in your early bipolar life when you are not capable of anything but limited life. Eat, drink and sleep, and I don't mean alcohol. Look after yourself and be gentle—you will come around. Face this thing with the luxury of pampering. At other times you will learn to be ruthless to kill your manic rising within you with anti-psychotics—but that will come later. Be patient and sleep and rest and take your medicine. Your sanity will return.

I have always enjoyed and needed to be in nature. It speaks to me and returns my sanity and balance. It resets my vision. I feel very affected by the modern rush to commercialize and advance. For me progress is walking through the rainforest and breathing clean air. It cleans the residue from my back. You may have a different place to reset your self. Perhaps you thrive in the busy metropolis. The busy-ness and confusion sets your soul to placid.

It is your responsibility to know what sets you straight and to go there. You have to do this on your own. You can build a huge support network but you alone have to do certain things. No one else knows you deep enough to do it for you. A doctor's actions alone will not fix you.

It used to crack me up when I flipped from a manic and psychotic tendency to a depressive and suicidal tendency. I would call my doctor and get an appointment for three weeks from today. Hello, I am suicidal and in mixed states. Looking back on it, perhaps I did not communicate well. But I was the sick one, I don't ever remember hearing anything about emergency protocol. They were all calm when my life was in danger.

To remedy this, I learned to predict my changing situation and, with my doctor, build a toolkit of medication for different purposes. It took time. I hope it takes less time for you.

A challenge in writing this book is to not come across as high and mighty and sounding pretentious. I strive to be naked and exposed in what I have seen, heard, and experienced. I am not perfect and I still struggle with bipolar. Mostly, I struggle with me.

A danger of tracking your journey in your logbook is to cross into hypergraphia. It can take you on a meaningless tangent. Be aware of the ego and lost time involved in this pursuit of writing copious amounts. I have had times where I had to limit myself. I needed to eat or drink or rest and I was consumed by the drive to write. Most of it turned out to be meaningless drivel. But at the time of writing, the divine muse is direct within and you'd better get it all down.

The important aspect of your diagnosis is what you are going to do with it. Are you aware? Do you own it? Do you believe it? Are they right? What are the details of your specific patterns?

Another tricky part of writing this book is to speak to our wide range: the number one, the suicidal; to the number ten, the manic psychotic. It is hard to believe that all the stages can be lived by the same person. And I need not give you any crazy ideas. You are responsible for your life and existence. You are the creator of your attitude and environment. Own it.

Will you pull a Christopher Reeve with me and face this challenge? What is our cure? Do we need more research? Do we need a new drug?

I believe we can do it now. This illness forced me to get to know myself in scary ways. I have to accept my weird actions and thoughts and feelings. It's all right. I'm human. I have been messed up. But I got better, and continue to. I am not perfect but I'm trying to tame this manic-depressive creature to be my pony ride. I want to train it to take me places I want to be. I grew tired of listening to it boss me around. It is now my servant.

I am the best I can be this day. I diagnose myself to need vegetables and fruit. I need to be kind to my thoughts. I need to play good tapes in my head and throw out those old ones that keep me down. I am not Jesus or Mohammed or Satan but I am a special person that can live to have good effects on my world. I am not better than everyone but I am unique and special.

I am responsible for me, and my diagnoses. I choose to get through this and move on. I desire to get to the point in this illness to open the gift that it can be. Bipolar is opening doors for me to enter and I am running through them. Sure I run into walls but who doesn't who is living life?

I for one do not want to be a senior who has watched television for decades. Life is a sport. Bipolar is a mean dirty coach that throws us into the mix. It can be brutal. Put me in coach. I'll learn to reduce the negatives of bipolar and grow the positive.

Points of thought and action:

#1 What is bipolar? (Continue to do my research.)

#2 Why am I bipolar?

#3 Start my number 1-10 chart—simply write the numbers on a calendar or however I want to document my chart.

#4 Accept responsibility for my thoughts, actions, and life.

#5 Be honest with myself and my doctor.

#6 (My personal plan.)

YOU MIGHT BE BIPOLAR

Here are a few scenarios that might help you discover if you might be bipolar. I tried to keep it on the lighter side.

If you were talking on your cell phone at the same time as reading a magazine and driving... you might be Bipolar.

If the people around you wear sunglasses because the colors of your clothing are that bright... you might be Bipolar.

If you can't continue your pornography bender because your credit cards are maxed out... you might be Bipolar.

If you discover that you have been smoking cigarettes for a while... you might be Bipolar.

If nobody but you thinks that your business idea is amazing... you might be Bipolar.

If everyone around you thinks you're Bipolar but you don't... you might be Bipolar.

If you bought 21 hats in an afternoon... you might be Bipolar.

If you booked a bus for a tour you're planning... you might be Bipolar.

If you invent something that no one appreciates... you might be Bipolar.

If you find yourself watching sunrises from a height of land... you might be Bipolar.

If you have prescription medication you don't feel you need to take... you might be Bipolar.

If the police have come to take you away... you might be Bipolar.

If you are an observer of the actual Big Bang... you might be Bipolar.

If you are playing guitar and singing to a stranger... you might be Bipolar.

If you suddenly find yourself to be Jesus Christ... you might be Bipolar.

If you are giving your family heirlooms to strangers... you might be Bipolar.

If you don't think there is anything wrong with you... you might be Bipolar.

If your phone bill is more than your rent... you might be Bipolar.

If you attempted to run a marathon, and you don't run... you might be Bipolar.

If you find yourself talking complete strangers into giving you rides... you might be Bipolar.

If you are chosen to save the world... you might be Bipolar.

If you can process and absorb multiple conversations at the same time... you might be Bipolar.

If you can sell goods and services to people... you might be Bipolar.

If you have tried the impossible and proven it to still be impossible... you might be Bipolar.

If you need to create things... you might be Bipolar.

If you can't sit down... you might be Bipolar.

If you interrupt others... you might be Bipolar.

If you make more money than others... you might be Bipolar.

If you book a trip to the South Pole... you might be Bipolar.

If you book a spot to space... you might be Bipolar.

If you already traveled to space without any ship... you might be Bipolar.

If you can time travel... you might be Bipolar.

If people say that you have potential... you might be Bipolar.

If you get bored... you might be Bipolar.

If you find yourself to be more productive than others... you might be Bipolar.

If you have expensive taste... you might be Bipolar.

If your brain feels like it is moving so fast that it is smoking... you might be Bipolar.

If you find that you are making more friends... you might be Bipolar.

If you only want to spend time by yourself... you might be Bipolar

If your dreams are preferred over your reality... you might be Bipolar.
If you have no interest in sex... you might be Bipolar.
If you don't enjoy anything... you might be Bipolar.
If you hate talking to people... you might be Bipolar.

Can you add some to this list?

HOPE AND SUICIDE

Have you visited the Suicidal Islands? I found them to be a one way ticket with no resort in sight, and no provided return transportation. I had to struggle to secure some means to return home.

It can suck you down and wither your juice. We see with only cave vision. I love the way Sylvia Plath describes her attempt under the house in, *The Bell Jar*. The whole world is above and around her; they search for her, she can hear them yet the thing within her has hidden her close to home, but a world away.

We need to fight back with inspiration and a desire for life. You need to be an expert in having and growing hope. You need to study and make hope chests of reasons to live and be happy—make a cache of great things that give you hope and purpose and joy. It could be nice pictures, letters, or things and places you need to do or visit. Have fun and take it seriously—your life could depend on it.

Write yourself coaching notes of what to do to get better. You have to do this and visit here before you kill yourself—remember to keep the carrot out there. Put in a full media package: music, a movie, a recording that you custom made, a book, cards, photographs of your loved ones that you cannot leave behind, snack packaging, a travel brochure, spiritual teachings, bible verses, quotes of inspiration. This is your hope chest of fullness—it can be as large or as small as you need.

This building of hope is essential to all of us and if you visit the suicidal realms it is a must, and more so, if you also have mixed states. You need to wage war on this illness because it will take you—it can throw you out of a moving car at seventy miles per hour. We need to be proactive to build our hope—this can be our last line of defense.

If you have nothing, absolutely zero to live for and you have the drive and energy to kill yourself, you just might. Reach for your hope chest before you get there and pull your socks up. Lift your feet up and run a few steps from the altar—it is not a place of glory or goodness. It can fool you into thinking that pulling the trigger or taking the bottle of pills is your only choice and it is out of love for your family. What a crock. What will it require for you to take bipolar seriously? It can mess you up badly, to the point where suicide is a bright light.

Prevent your extremes, prevent your extremes, and prevent your extremes. The odd time, mistaken thinking can take control and you have no power left in your mind to counter the suicide call. For this reason we need to create defenses with the hope chest and train your mind to think, think, and to always think. The more you think and retrain your mind to be disciplined to think and play different tapes and to act differently, the safer you will be. We have to take the offensive role with bipolar—we have to beat it down when we have the chance.

Are you taking it seriously? Do you intend to do the exercises at the chapter ends of this book or are you more interested in what is on TV? You have to try. Does what I write about make you angry? Sometimes I find the things that make me angry have something to teach me. I can't do it for you. Whenever you can make progress in disciplining your mind, you need to. There may come times when you are seemingly controlled by psychosis and the numbing of medication. Any self-control that you can muster may be a life saver. This is your basic training to wage and win war on bipolar, and you are not simply going to survive, you are going to take bipolar prisoner and make it work for you.

You can and will suffer more and die. You may not die, and driving into that overpass will just paralyze you from the neck down. Borrow hope until you have some of your own. Come on, get out of that fatalistic thinking and build some hope. Even a small spark will save you. And if you have no hope you better get your butt around other people's hope. Stop doing the things that make you feel bad—your life depends on stopping and learning. If you want a new life, you need to leave your old ways behind.

We are each unique in what gives us hope. What is your inspiration? Listen to a certain piece of music. Call a crisis line. Go to church or mosque or temple. Go to an addictions support group. Call a friend or family. Walk in the mountains once a summer. Maybe you need to help less fortunate people. We should not compare ourselves to others but it can be useful to help someone that is worse off—it can kick out your self-pity. You may come away full of hope and wanting to live.

I reacted to thoughts of suicide by simply putting it off till the next day. I would never do it this day and this alone, if you could follow it like I did, will always place it in the future. Like A.A., "A Day at a Time." After I had been through it a few times I knew that it would pass after a time and I would get better. I put it off and waited.

The best defense is an offence and by reducing my highs and killing them, I reduced my lows and suicidal depth. What do you need to prevent your suicidal state?

There were a few years when I had little involvement with women and a reason I had to live was so I could make love with a woman again. I could kill myself only after I slept with another woman. In my suicidal time this worked because I repelled people. In my manic times this was dangerous because I could go there and get it done. If you use this approach of you can't kill yourself before doing something, you'd better make it the near impossible and, better yet, something that, if you do it, will be a sign of a better life for you and you will no longer want to kill yourself.

Don't write a suicide note: write a plan of action that you will follow when you find yourself in that state. You should have folders built to utilize in your bipolar remedy. An example could say: It is all right that I feel suicidal and want to do this; I am not the only one. It is part of bipolar. It will pass. I will not do it this day. I will rebuild my hope by opening my hope chest and reviewing it—this will give me a glimmer of hope and if it does not work I will call___ and visit____ to borrow their hope. I will do three of my favorite things:... I will forgive myself. I will not linger here. I will strive for balance and learn to live there.

I will not leave a mess for my loved ones to clean up (this always helped me.) What if it doesn't work and I leave myself paralyzed? I will not commit suicide. I refuse to become a statistic. I choose to reach for my gift. I am worthy and deserve a good life of peace and joy. If none of this works, I will put it off till tomorrow, and then do the try-everything plan again and then put it off till tomorrow...

You might want to include things that you have done that have made a difference in people's lives. It is up to you to build your suicide hope kit in the way that will work for you. Suicide is never a solution—learn to prevent it. Be open-minded and you will have your own solutions. You will get to the place of avoiding the realm altogether—you will build your new life to not include suicidal ideation.

It is great to leave the Suicide Islands. It is weird but in a small way I miss my suicidal days. It is a perverse narcissistic pride, an ego thing. It can be twisted glory, and a place of wisdom to know true values. It is a place that I strive to ignore and avoid. You can do the same. Maintain your hope and fan the flames. This is your life to build and live in excellence. Be easy on yourself and gentle in learning and striving.

It takes time—reach out to help others: you will be helping yourself too. A.A. talks about the best way to stay sober being to help someone else stay sober. We can stay sane and alive by helping others stay sane and alive.

Without hope we are dead. With hope and vision we live in truth and beauty. I have vision for your life to be of health and balance and peace and joy and communion with others. You can do it.

Points of thought and action:
#1   What are my suicidal tendencies?
#2   What keeps me from doing it?
#3   How can I grow those preventatives?
#4   How can I prevent those depths of depression?
#5   How do I build and fill my hope chest?
#6   (My personal plan.)

INLETS

An inlet is anything that inputs your person with good, bad or neutral influences. It can be food, drink, music, crowds, nature, people, work, media, or the weather. Life is stress, or change: it can be good, bad or indifferent. To live life is to have little curveballs continually thrown at you.

Our job is to know how certain things affect our moods—everything has the potential to. How does each and every thing you are exposed to change you for the better or worse? It sounds tedious but it is vital in reducing illness.

We need to be aware of our inlets and how they affect us. I would suggest making lists and taking this seriously. If you get nothing else from this book, this is what I want you to get a grasp of—it will catch all things. It covers our medication, our friends and our activities. It applies to our thinking. What are your inlets and how do they affect you?

This will empower you to be aware. Our world is cause and effect—sometimes we have no idea and there are things that are beyond our control, but we can regain control quickly if we know how to reset our thinking, actions, and emotions with positive inputs.

It is our power to develop and change the way we live each moment. Make small changes and be conscious of what is going on and you will gain power to live your life. Feel and imagine it, think it and dream it, and you will live it. A small step becomes repeated as an automatic step that becomes even larger in its scope and affect.

In your charting of how everything affects you, please keep in mind how it changes with you, your mood and situation of bipolar. We are complex beings. Are we introvert or extrovert? Are we passive or aggressive? I have trouble answering personality questions with one pat answer because bipolar has developed in me a paradoxical personality.

Uncontrolled bipolar can be a negative monster, but with refining and discipline we can have deeper experiences of ourselves, and the world. I can relate to a much wider range of people, having gone through what I have.

Inlet awareness is integral to living in your gift. It is your key to reducing and eliminating your illness. Inlet management can reduce your dependence on the medical system and medication. If you reduce things that cause your anxiety, it is simple to accept that you will need less medication for your anxiety. (Cause and effect.)

If your doctor does not understand that you need less medication because you have reduced your inlets of stressors, our medical system needs more help than I think. Certain people will make your awareness lists. At specific times of your mood, you may not be able to be around certain people: when you are a little manic that person irritates and angers you—there is nothing good about spending time with them. And hopefully there are certain people that are great inlets for you all the time. When you spend time with them, it steadies and calms you, and makes you laugh.

Our ultimate goal is to install more positive inlets into our thinking and emotions and to reduce the negative ones. This one pursuit alone will empower you. What makes you feel good or great? Do more of that and less of what upsets you and makes you feel negative. It is simple—why don't more of us do it?

Once again, I know I need to exercise. And I think most of us need to move our bodies to live best. There are few people that can get away emotionally and mentally by not exercising. Many of us are so deep in a rut that we think we cannot move through exercise to a better place. And we can find doctors and professionals who will enable us in this sedate festering. I get aches and pains if I do not exercise: if I looked hard enough I could find a doctor who would encourage me to not exercise and to take his or her prescriptions.

Increase the size and number of your positive inlet pipes and you will be a happier person. This is a proactive approach. You put good things into a car and it will work better. The same is true for you. We each have unique positive inlets. Maybe you like opera or punk music or picking up garbage—anything goes. The important thing is for you to know and use this to enhance your life.

The answer does not sit waiting in one pill, the pill can help but so can anything—it all adds up to your personal solution. Some of you are not ready to hear this, and apply it. I would encourage you to take in what you can and apply a few principles and leave the rest. Come back later and chances are you will be able to take in more.

I would like for this book to be a starting point for you to develop your own guidebook. You know what you need, it takes practice and you can do it. Write your own book of what works for you. In the process of writing, you will increase your distance from illness. Your techniques to health and the gift will be solidified. It will be a solid tool for your review. Light will be shone on your path.

The number of times that I have surprised doctors with my awareness of how a drug affects me is disappointing. "This sleeping pill took away my ability for R.E.M. sleep." "You could tell that?"

The doctor model is somewhat based on their diagnoses and remedy of our situation. We can tell them some symptoms but they prefer to do the interview and tests and let the empirical evidence speak to their mode of diagnoses. All of this is great but where are we in the picture? I believe we are the greatest force available for our healing and good health.

We need to be experts at how things affect us. Everything. It gets easier with time to be aware. Yet things change too. If we are alert we continually get training subjects. I used to like commercials on TV—I despise them now and have to avoid them. At times I can and cannot talk to certain friends on the phone.

How does music affect you? Each category of music will tend to do different things to you. There may be exceptions to every rule you find. Classical music is perfect for my overstressed mind at times. It soothes my excessive thinking. But sometimes I put it on and it is wrong and I don't know why, but I can feel it. I like heavy metal and punk on occasion—they tend to get me motivated and moving. Sometimes it is wrong and it just angers me and I have to change it or turn it off entirely. I used to be very narrow-minded musically but I have found that with age, exposure, and bipolar, I can appreciate most everything on occasion. There are certain categories that are more predictable for me with certain effects. What are your tendencies?

Have fun with your inlets: you could draw cartoon pictures of yourself and your inlets. What may seem strange to some people can be the greatest thing for us. We should strive to be open and try things until we prove them to be not beneficial.

I promise that if you reduce your negative inlets you will reduce the illness; and if you fatten your positive inlets you will also reduce the illness and be building your gift side.

Points of thought and action:
#1 What are the inlet stressors that affect my mood?
#2 How do these change with depression and mania?
#3 What are my negative stressors and how do I reduce their power and frequency?
#4 What are my positive stressors and how do I increase their power and frequency?
#5 Which types of media affect me in what ways?
#6 (My personal plan.)

PROCESSING

If you are anything like me, you can take in much stimuli. Your brain sucks in the experiences and information like a sponge, but it can take its toll. How much can we reasonably take in and process or have outlets for? We need to monitor our intake amounts in order to safely process. The pace of events can be too quick to keep our internal balance.

We need to reflect on our life as it occurs; we may need to talk to our friends, we may need to journal. A long walk to think may be our ticket to internal peace. I like to think about what is going on but there is a certain point where I have too much pressure and it is simply a matter of releasing the pressure through outlets. I cannot keep it inside any longer. I have to shut down my intake of stimuli and especially the negative. I may even have to restrict my positive intake pipes until I process the excess within me.

I have intense curiosity and interest in a wide range of subjects. I love to look at things from different perspectives—it is a great way to pass time to try and figure out why things are the way they are and why people do the things they do. Yet I have a tendency to over analyze events and situations.

Sometimes I get to the point where I cannot shut it off. I have to restrict my inlets of stimulus input and choke down what I have. I can get in a real analyzing rut that serves no purpose. I have to learn better to accept things as they are on occasion when my mind is smoking. I have to divert my attention to simpler concerns.

How we process a certain situation is how we turn the same circumstances into positive or negative. The same event can happen to two of us and we will have different judgment decisions of how it will affect us. Is your bottle of pills half full or empty? Two people have bipolar and one commits suicide and the other uses bipolar to rise to the top of her field—two vastly different outcomes with the same problem to overcome.

I heard a brain specialist talk about teenagers and their inability to listen to simple advice to avoid danger. This man claimed that many teens simply have to experiment and try things for themselves—it is their brain makeup at that age that forces this approach. Some couldn't listen to your advice even if they wanted to. It can be useful in leaving your upbringing and building a life of your own. For some that try and make big mistakes, their life is over—drinking and driving could be an example. As teens with bipolar we need to strive to be extra diligent to work through the illness. Get out of any rut as soon as you can. Take your medication. Beware of falling into patterns.

We all face unique challenges in life. The type of mind we have will affect how we approach difficulties. We have to face our decisions and not procrastinate: we can train ourselves to make decisions quicker and face something that needs to be addressed and not prolong the mental torment of procrastinating.

We each learn differently: reading, listening, doing, being guided, struggling on our own, or a combination. You have your own unique ways of learning. How do you learn? Some of you can read a book such as this and readily apply its principles to leave your illness stage and enter your gift life.

Others of you need to try things on your own and cannot learn from reading. Or you can read and you have to change the content to be your own. You might have to make recordings to emphasize your learning to absorb. No method of learning is any better than any other—we are each different and it is our responsibility to know which methods of learning for us are natural and which are struggles. I believe that we can develop new ways of learning to enhance our ability to learn. Bipolar has developed me into a hands on doer / maker, and spatial thinking learner.

Because our classrooms have been set up to cater to certain learning styles, we handicap certain individuals who don't learn in the oral and written. Also, our medical model is based on oral language. If listening and speaking are challenges, the way our doctors are trained is also a handicap for us. Have medical professionals ever given you a test to discover how you learn best? Perhaps colleges and universities should be teaching adaptive approaches to medical personnel to reach us through our needed learning approaches.

Your parents ideally should help you know how you learn best but ultimately we must figure it out. We have the most to gain and the most to lose in life. If you get to the level of mastery of how you learn and are able to apply it, look out; you will be a force to reckon with, whether it is in leaving your illness or knowing how to do your job or run your business. You may find yourself needing a more challenging position in life.

One of the reasons I enjoy the pursuit of writing is the challenge. My head can be a needy place to dwell and in writing I face my brain all the time. It can be tough, and a breeze—it is always different. Living with bipolar has left me with overcoming skills, it challenged me for my very life and I find that, now when I am living in relative balance, I need challenges. I can plateau and become blah. I need to present myself with new experiences to fully engage. The ultimate challenge of facing down psychosis and suicide has left me with an edge for survival; a void that needs to be a pioneer, an explorer, an adventurer.

To keep my life in balance I need to experience adventure sports. I need to whitewater canoe or mountain bike once in a while to feel right. Surfing in the canoe on the river or ocean hits the spot. A job of mine was to deal with deadly gas and breathing air equipment—it engages me fully to be challenged by my surroundings. The challenge is to pursue these inlets in a safe manner.

The fact of too many stimuli was my greatest problem to counter and remedy—sometimes it is best to eliminate certain exposures. There are certain events that I attend that are guaranteed to make me high. A good upbeat event with socializing is a sure recipe: throw in some music, look out. I had to stop going to certain places because they drove me manic. I am much more resilient now that I am older. I have built good outlets to release the excess angst and energy.

I never expected, after the illness of bipolar vacated, to miss the challenge and the survival-seeking. You may have this and you may have different results from leaving your illness behind. The monsters and ghosts will come out and play in your mind and relationships and life. It may keep you really busy for your whole life just to keep the illness tied up at bay. And others of us can sink the boat and drown the illness forever and live fully in our gift.

We can gain mastery over this bipolar through processing. You may have to use your counselor and group and other methods to optimize your internal processing. Processing is a key to bringing all the components to strength. What do you need this very moment to achieve your balance? We need to study and apply logic: if this occurs, then this will follow. If I am agitated and ingest caffeine, agitation increases. If I am agitated and exercise and breathe and play good loops in my head, agitation decreases.

You will have to burn up the negative in you somehow—you can write or talk or paint or mow the grass. Clean the bathroom or organize the closet. Action can focus our mental energy and cast the negative to the side. We can choose to be affected less by our family. We have to process the negatives in our lives to control them and make choices instead of allowing them to control us.

In the past, you might have performed a burning ritual. You don't fully understand why you had to burn those items. It can symbolize a new start. It purges the past and the connection we had to it. Take the positive out of it and advance.

We have to refine and build more of the good to attract the good inlets. We can crystallize our absorption and develop new ways of learning. We can live in a new way. We need to reward ourselves for the good: the exercise, the learning about medication, and the compliance. We need to celebrate our achievements.

I promise that the harder you work at this, the more progress you will eventually make. You may have to struggle for years and then you will break through and momentum will carry you.

It is our adventure that we process and harness and train. Play in your mind: your imagination is powerful to change your experience. You could imagine that you develop your life outcome like photography—you imagine your desired outcomes and then you take the steps in shooting the film and processing it to negative and choose the paper to print your beautiful pictures. Or it could be a digital camera and you press delete to remove the unwanted.

Have fun with your imagination concerning your learning and changing your life. Make a game of it and this may be a key to your success. We don't celebrate our lives enough. Have a party to celebrate your coming out of hospital, or not going into the hospital. Have fun processing and developing your life.

Points of thought and action:

#1   How do I process my mind when it is swimming with events and people?

#2   Do I have to decrease my stimulus at times?

#3   Can I clean my head out with talking, walking, writing, creating, or cleaning?

#4   Do I learn best by reading, listening, doing, or observing?

#5   What do I need this moment to achieve my balance?

#6   (My personal plan.)

OUTLETS

There were times in my illness days when I was unable to do much of anything: it was primarily eat and sleep. I had to learn to allow myself to be in a simple state of recovery. It was in other times when I had energy and the power to choose that I learned that certain outlets were better for me than others.

I studied some basic power engineering and a main thrust of it is to have pressure relief valves. Back in the early days of using boilers thousands of people were killed with explosions. Safety measures were developed to keep the water level adequate and allow built up pressure to release.

We, as a society, do not teach our children to let off their steam. We react and command our children to simply control themselves, but we need to work at developing individualized methods with them to self-control their build up of pressure. Anger concerns and frustrations may lead to many of our problems—who are you and how do you need to live differently to achieve better results?

Some of us have the good fortune to have pursuits that allow us to vent. Sports are great and your awareness of when to let loose with activity is important. Then the actual motivating yourself to do it is paramount.

For some people that do not have healthy pressure releases, extreme boozing and drugging are the chosen methods. We know that they can bring their own set of problems. What works for you? Do you like to dance? Make crafts? I found stitching leatherwork to be relaxing.

I am in rough shape if I do not use my outlets: I will deteriorate and have to use more medication. For me, exercise and movement are great.

I play guitar to unwind on occasion, it is great to pound the strings or pluck them gently; it soothes my soul. I watch movies—they rest my body and relax my mind. Depending on the movie it can appease my psychotic side or uplift or motivate. They can inspire me or bring me down. Depending on my state, a sad or downer movie can counter my mania, if I can sit still.

List your possible outlets: they could be watching TV, cooking, drawing a picture, throwing darts, solving crossword puzzles, shooting a bow and arrow, playing video games. Go to the spa, have a bath, treat yourself.

The great thing is to remember that you control your choice and length of outlet. It is another one of your tools that you have to balance your life and symptoms. This simple awareness and use of outlets can reduce and eliminate your hospital time. Medication itself can be an outlet to open you up to relaxation and allow you to live better.

Continue to know your inlets to restrict the negative and increase the positive. Stay aware of how this can all fluctuate as you change. If you have been living in illness, it may surprise you how much your life will flourish in the next five years.

It blows me away that I no longer get bothered by my, usual manic time of the year. I am married and happy. I approach my gift years and live the best I can with gratitude. I am still surprised on occasion when bipolar raises its ugly side for me to deal with, but these are minor events, now that I have developed techniques and experience.

A main reason I have left my illness years behind is that I've achieved competency in this inlet, process, and outlet system. A certain pursuit can work as both inlet and outlet—what does the activity leave you feeling like? I continue to tweak my methods to my changing needs and surroundings. Life is change. If you don't adapt with it, you may be left in the bitter dust. Death is waiting and I want to live the most that I can. I want to live large and enjoy my inlets and outlets.

I need to paddle my canoe in the estuary and hear and see the birds and seals. I need to write, and be taken up in the world I create and follow the characters through. My outlets save me. Watching TV can be an outlet for me at times—I think I use it more for a numbing device to help with the processing. I watch and it dulls my stimulus senses. I tend to watch TV that makes me laugh—laughter is great for everything.

Laughter is great power: learn to laugh at yourself and your actions. It will help you to let go of certain things and it will temper your priorities to realize what truly matters. We cannot carry the anger from this morning with us throughout the day, it will poison our entire existence. Laugh about the driver that cut you off. Listen to and watch comedy. Make comedy. Learn jokes and tell them. Laugh and be funny. Take yourself less seriously. We can get pretty intense: to see the lighter side is a gift.

The greatest thing we can do in this outlet department is to cultivate a great attitude and approach. We need to listen to what we need at any given time. What do you need right now to counter the stress and change of your life? You might be helped to take up knitting or making music. You might need to talk to people. What are your outlets of recreation and entertainment? Do you need to change and adapt them to your different needs?

Be aware of your outlets. Maybe your venting with swearing and yelling needs to be changed. Learn about anger management—talk to your people and adapt. Maybe you need to find a different job to deal with your horrible commute, maybe it is worth it to wake up an hour early to avoid the rush hour. You could sit at work and relax and meditate—you could learn Spanish in your wait and face your day with a fresh approach. Maybe you have to leave the city for more serenity or move to the city for more stimuli.

We don't want to keep the bad inside and outlets are our tools to let the negative out. Sewage treatment is a great thing before releasing it into our rivers and oceans—it can affect our environment. If we have good outlets we can limit the damage to ourselves; the negative will be shipped out in a sustainable manner that hurts no one including ourselves. And sweet good water will be made with our good outlets.

This is your life and your gift to live well.

Points of thought and action:
#1   What builds up in me that needs release?
#2   Are there certain events that I need to avoid?
#3   What are my positive outlets?
#4   Do I need to exercise more often?
#5   What do I need to do right now to achieve a healthier balance?
#6   (My personal plan.)

THE GOOD AND THE BAD
DOCTOR

I hope that your doctor is amazing; that he or she takes the time to communicate with you and explain what to expect. It is frightening to lose your self and to think and act differently—we need as much support and encouragement as we can muster and stumble upon.

We live in a busy world and doctors tend to be pulled in many directions. We have to remember that they are human and are affected by some of the same things that we are. They also run a business. I believe they should be paid well: it is a tough job to have that much responsibility, and they have devoted years of their life to their education. They earn my respect and admiration.

Years ago, I found psychiatrists to be out there a little further in their idiosyncrasies—they are in wards hidden away and working in a field that few are called to. It seemed to draw some odd people. In some cases it is not hard to see it is about the money or power. Is your doctor all-powerful? This was the general consensus a few decades back. Do we heal better if we believe in their mighty touch? Yes, I would agree. They are powerful healers in your life. Yet I believe that you and I have even greater power in our lives for good and bad. We are the ones that act full time in our heads and bodies and lives. Still, many people undermine their doctor's power with self-sabotage.

Early in my career I was exposed to a doctor who was basic—he missed major points to prevent my manic episodes, and he overmedicated. He liked to keep his ward full of patients. He did not empower me in the least to get through bipolar. If I had stayed with this doctor I would not be as healthy as I am today. He was the doctor and I was the patient. He knew what was best for me. He saw me for two to three minutes per day when I was hospitalized and sporadically when I was not in hospital. He was afraid to put me on anti-depressants because they would send me high. I went high anyway and he did nothing to prevent the highs. In retrospect I was another body to fill the bed and his office on occasion.

I have had several doctors since: you can tell what motivates them, what their priorities are and how skillful they are in treating someone. It's true that you can only treat someone who wants to be treated. Part of my situation was who I am. I like responsibility—my parents grilled it into me early. I needed a doctor that recognized and used my responsibility for good.

I despise the power game of some doctors; it is my opinion that I have more power to heal myself than they do to heal me—especially in the mentally ill realm. They have as much power as we grant with the living out of our everyday existence, in our good and bad decisions. Yes, the medications are important and essential. Doctors have the goods; the pharmaceuticals can and will save us.

My annual cycle of mania and then my slide into depression caused me to experience withdrawal from major tranquilizers every year. It was tough. I never remember a doctor educating me on the effects of withdrawing from a major tranquilizer. Depending on the substance and then having it gone is a severe trial to go through.

Under my first doctor's care, I felt myself slipping high and all I had was Lithium. I had nothing to lose, I was turning psychotic and could not get to the doctor immediately. I took progressively heavier amounts of Lithium. I do not recommend this use. It messed with my electrolytes and I felt like a bag of chalk.

Later Lithium caused my thyroid gland to shut down. It may be connected to my overdose. This doctor wanted me to stay on Lithium and to take Synthroid for my gland. The Lithium did not help in my mood stabilization. Perhaps this guy wanted me to be more messed up to make a good dependent patient. I don't remember the frequency of his blood work to monitor the effects of the Lithium.

I could go on and on with bad stories of bad doctors—but that will compound the effect. I believe in the law of attraction. (reference #3)

Whatever you focus on you will receive more of. Maybe it was I who attracted those results.

Only you and I can bring out the best that is in a doctor. Yes, I know we shouldn't have to. But this is the way of life. It isn't fair. A doctor is human and may accept your predictable negative patterns. The doctor may give up on you: you will only go so far.

I believe in self-fulfilled prophecies. Do you really want to get through this illness? Have you accepted your place in life? Do you like the attention? Is it your way of getting back at your parents? Is it where you want to be? Do you like your doctor? Do you hate your doctor?

Have you ever been honest with your doctor? Can your doctor trust you? Are you true to your word? Do you take the illness seriously? Have you worked through your addiction tendencies? Does your doctor know about your self-medicating: your drinking, and your street drugging? How do your addiction issues progress with your prescription medication? Do you tell your doctor that you supplement your treatment plan with a forty of vodka every month end? Your doctor is there to help you.

Overmedicating, undermedicating, the wrong medication, side effects, and withdrawal can be problems. Many of these drugs are highly addictive. Because of this and that our western medical world runs on prescriptions, I believe that many of us are on a little too much drug. It is a seductive road.

Bless your doctor if she asked you how much coffee you drink, and if you exercise, before writing a prescription for an anti-anxiety drug. I am here to tell you it is part of you getting better to change your lifestyle. Maybe your body and mind are telling you something about the way you live your life. Do you watch TV all day and night and never exercise and then accept the doctor's signing another sleeping pill prescription?

Maybe you could ask your doctor if you should start walking with the goal to walk more and more, and maybe ride a bike, or swim; and maybe the doctor would encourage you to cut your sleeping medication by a quarter. Do you drink caffeine in the last half of the day?

There is much information out there about getting to sleep. If you are on sleeping medication and have not been informed about proper sleep habits by your doctor, I'm sorry but your doctor, for whatever reason, cares more about writing that prescription and getting you out the door than you getting a good night's sleep. The point is you are responsible for your life. Your doctor is your doctor—they can only do

so much. We can blame your doctor or your kindergarten teacher—
your choice. You have to live with yourself to face the mirror and the
pillow. We have to make choices to enhance our doctor's ability to make
us the healthiest bipolar we can be.

It starts with communication. You have to be honest. No secrets
about your drugs. If you are saving up your sleeping medication for
three days in a row to binge on, you hurt yourself and your loved ones.
Your doctor hopefully cares about you, but another patient will enter
his office after you leave. When you deceive your doctor you deceive
yourself. Some of this book will seem so basic to you who are already
on your way, I'm glad for you. Others of us wreck our lives and then
blame others.

I have seen a psychiatrist after a patient committed suicide—I could
tell that this would taint this individual's life. These doctors really care
about their people. Part of our problems stem from us not caring enough
about ourselves. Our society does not major in teaching us how to look
after ourselves. We need to teach, from an earlier age, responsibility for
our actions and health.

Living with bipolar is an adult pursuit—some of our parents did
not raise us to be independent adults, sometimes because their parents
passed the same issues on to them. This is our day to face our true selves.
Cause equals effect. Being honest with your doctor is vital for your life.
We need to discover how we learn best and help our doctor help us.

Several of us go to the doctor's and whine and focus on the non-
important issues. To empower a doctor to be the best they can be,
we need to be the best we can be. Imagine sitting in their chair: their
patient went off medication once again. God told him to do it. It had
taken a year to get the patient straightened out: he wasn't even on much
medication; the patient said there were no side effects. Everything was
clear sailing, the patient went off his medication without consulting the
doctor and now he is even more messed up.

If you want the gift side of this illness long term, you need to
work with your doctor—onward and upward. If you are traveling
at all outside your doctor's range, ask your doctor to write a letter of
introduction for you, mention your level of responsibility with your
bipolar and list your medications and freedoms with them—just in case
you need to see someone or be hospitalized.

This can really help in case you ditched your medication; you don't want a doctor starting from scratch again in case you can't remember or you can't talk from side-effects. If you have medications that work, you want to continue to use them. Consider a medical alert bracelet or necklace. I found that I had a fair bit of information that my doctor would convey in this letter. It gave me an extra sense of security and assurance that if I did have an episode, I would be taken care of with the right stuff. This would include any side-effect medication.

Sometimes we need to take nice trips on psychiatric medications and lie on the couch and watch a movie. "Yes doctor, the anti-psychotics are cleaning up my thoughts, I couldn't get off the sofa for a couple of days, and we might soon need to tone it down a bit." The next month your doctor may have reduced your tranquilizer and you have to get off the sofa and walk downtown and go for a swim. Think of how good you will feel after the swim. Yes, it is brutal to get moving. Put your wildest, fastest music on.

Some doctors are still stuck in the I DOCTOR AM GOD—you patient. You know nothing. I find compliance needs to have a built in trust and allegiance. I will not yield to a doctor anymore unless I do my own research and believe that doctor knows what he is doing. They have to earn my respect. I am an intelligent person who takes my life seriously.

In the beginning I trusted my doctors completely; I was innocent and struggled in communicating because this doctor had no time to converse. We tend to have to lean on our doctors more in the beginning stages of this illness. Educate yourself. Know your medications as in depth as your doctor does. Is she checking on the potential damage to your organs? Your pharmacist is an excellent resource. We cannot leave ourselves fully in the laps of any one person.

The magazines are always better in the next doctor's office. Be careful that you have exhausted all the good that can come out of this present doctor. Is it you that is not living up to the challenges? Be easy on yourself. Again we need to be nice, and assertive with ourselves at the same time, and know which way to lean—this takes time to develop.

You may never need to get another doctor in your life, that would be great; but if you move or need a new doctor, you need wisdom in your choices. Talk to your friends and family. You may have to educate your entire support network—they can be sticks in the mud that worship the godhood that is doctor. The people in your support network bring their own subjective experiences to you. Please be aware of their human factor.

If you are true to yourself and talk with your support group, you will know when it is time to change doctors. I believe that we can outgrow our doctors. Doctors are human and they may have us pegged as we are now and hold us back from better days. I am here to tell you that you can change to a better you. Please, if you are just hospitalized or in rough condition, lay low, take it all slow. Look after your basic needs. Please note that it is best to change doctors in times of your stability.

Your network has agreed that you have outgrown your doctor or she is not good enough for you, etc. Have you done your research as to who else is available and who would be the best for you? My best switch was in the same waiting room. My old doctor was always at least an hour late for my appointments and then he would talk about himself more than ask me questions. You can learn a lot from other patients. Open your ears and your eyes. The receptionist broadcasts information too.

Research your ideal new doctor. I am assuming this is in your best healthy time and you have the lucidity to carry this out. Sometimes you stumble upon a better doctor in time of emergency, for example a manic or suicidal entry into the hospital. You could be in another city and get a new doctor—this happened to me accidentally, with ultimate purpose. My new doctor did not overmedicate me and my manic hospital stay was reduced from six weeks to two. I was happy not to drop into as long of a depression.

This new doctor who helped me was only capable of carrying me so far—he was the one who talked about himself more than about me. Probably at the time I did not want to talk about me. Yes I like to hear about a doctor's experiences but where is the leadership? I am hard on myself and hard on my doctors. You have to be to get out of the illness.

Planning and predictability are quite often thrown out the window with bipolar. The subject of bipolar is not a black and white subject. Your personal gray area will be different from mine. Remember that it is your life that you are fighting for—if you need to stay with the same doctor and work through your addiction or honesty issues, work at it like your life depends on it. We may have places of similarity—we can celebrate that and gain courage for our own gray backwood places, may we shed light on them. Your life is special and unique and needs to be lived like nobody else.

Along with your continuing research about bipolar, in times when you can think straight, you should be planning things you need to improve on. Talk to your counselor and friends. Develop ideas to strengthen your weak areas—we all have them. Perhaps with your new doctor you want to take the step of giving up your highs. Your old doctor and you have had too much bad history together and you are going nowhere. You are finally at the place where you are willing to give up those great highs: after living in suicidal depression, those highs can seem like a bright place you want to go to.

Your doctor would be impressed with this point on your agenda to get better. Where else can you go together? Back to school? That business? Reduce your medication? Try a new medication? That creative pursuit? Back to your marriage? Into being single? What do you need to do? You can do it a step at a time with the right support and persistence. Your doctor can open real doors with you. Take the relationship with your doctor seriously—you can set the tone and gain your full life in leaps and bounds.

Make a list of areas you would like to make progress on. Not only will this impress your new or present doctor, it is a strong step toward making the change in your life. This life with bipolar can be war at times, a battle against our mind and the world. To wage war to win we need the counsel of many to succeed.

Make a plan with your doctor to reach the goals on your list. Perhaps less of a stone-over in the morning from your sleeping medication: your doctor reviews your sleep hygiene with you. You agree to not use caffeine after a certain time and to exercise and do your own research into sleep. Your doctor agrees that you will do your part and he will allow you to take three quarters of your old dose of sleeping pill. You wake up refreshed and new, you start your day earlier, mentally you are alert and physically you are active sooner and wearing yourself out to sleep better. You see your doctor next time and your life has improved. It is amazing.

After a few months your doctor sees your improvements and suggests cutting your medication down further. Perhaps you rode your bicycle for five miles the day before and forgot to take your sleeping medication; you felt bad and told your doctor. He asked you how you slept. You had slept great, with wonderful dreams. In two years you are off your regular dose of sleeping medication and only take it on occasion when all else fails. Your lifestyle changes balance you out to a good sleep. You worked it through with your doctor. This is only one example of what does happen.

My first psychiatrist would not take my depression bottoms off with medication—he would not prevent my manic psychotic highs. He had several years to observe the pattern. Fast-forward several years with much suffering and tenacity: my saint psychiatrist empowered me to inject myself with a major tranquilizer. He had a nurse show me how to inject with an orange. I injected myself for a few seasons as a preventative and reduction in mania—it was scary yet empowering.

The first thing I did was to inject myself with a quarter to a third of what I used to receive, and I injected it twice as frequently. I was not over medicated on this huge mountain peak: I rode on these nice flat hills. And by month end, I was not withdrawing from the reduced tranquilizer in my muscle. I had the good coverage of the medication but not the negatives of too much and too little in my system.

After a few seasons I had my lifestyle set to who I needed to be and let go of the syringes. And I had to use them again ten years later.

You could look at the medical system of interdependence and monthly injections as the standard—is it best for the patient or is it to manage the patient? I agree there is a need for the latter. If a hundred bipolar people who used injections for mania management got their addictive tendency together and were empowered to do their own injections, how many would follow in my path and lose the injections entirely?

I am not saying that no one should be getting injections of tranquilizers—we should be receiving the proper amounts and perhaps smaller doses and more often. In my experience, this was a big step in regaining my life. If you took any hundred people and gave them the full monthly injection, it would take many good things from their lives in the first days of maximum dose. And by month end, they would be in the withdrawal valley, anxious for the next ride to peak.

I found with this approach that withdrawal was a piece of cake—the smaller doses did not seem to trigger the same dependency issues. And I was able to function and still have the blanket of tranquilizer in my system. But we are all different—talk to your doctor. This is one topic in this book that is sure to shake things up. Diabetics give their own injections, why not responsible mental health users?

I have no regrets about changing doctors. It can be a dangerous thing to do—you have to do it for the right reasons, and be honest. It is not usually worth it to be honest with your old doctor as to why you are moving on—they tend not to be open. What will you gain from an action or word? Cause and effect. Always think of how something said or done will effect changes.

You are responsible for your actions—although this is hard to swallow when you are out of your mind. Responsibility is the sturdiest path to living fully sane. Honesty with yourself and responsibility are your cornerstones.

Work with your doctor. Build trust. Doctors have your back. They save your life. They can also miss things that could kill you: be wary, but with your right mind, we need to cover all the potential problems with our doctor, and sometimes in advance. We have a tricky creature within us that can change our thoughts.

You will have the rest of your life to sort it out, but be careful of the dangerous areas that need to be addressed today. Use your times of good lucid thinking to learn what went wrong, and change your approach. This is a personal illness and we need unique solutions.

We need to take responsibility for our illness and life. Doctors are there to help us in this pursuit. With responsibility comes great freedom and challenge. Your doctor will help you rise to your gift. Open your arms to a better way of life.

Points of thought and action:

#1   What are my doctor's best and worst traits?

#2   What are my best and worst traits in interacting with my doctor?

#3   How can I improve my communication and responsibility?

#4   Do I have any addiction issues with my medications?

#5   What do I need and want to work on with my doctor?

#6   (My personal plan.)

TOOL KIT OF MEDICATION

Have you accepted your need for medication? A common theme for us is to go off our medication. We don't need it for many reasons: it isn't natural, the side effects are harmful. Do you still want to go off your medication?

I agree that drugs can be brutal. One time I was not on enough side effect medication and my spine and body rotated so my head felt like it would twist right off. I lost my ability to speak—yeah, I love verbal diarrhea when you cannot talk, very frustrating. I could not write notes fast enough.

I have felt the drugs lop my head off to sleep: I saw my eyelids appear black with stars blinking on and off. I have taken anti-psychotic medication and thankfully felt a mop gently soothing my ravaged mind, it massaged my burned out psychotic brain paths.

Every drug works differently, each has a specific purpose. Side effects vary. As time goes by the drugs are getting cleaner and better. I am thankful to live in this day and age. I never liked to be confined to a psychiatric ward for a few days, let alone wanting the permanent cage of the old days. I embrace the psychiatric drugs.

Some of the hell I went through in my bipolar career was due to the drugs the doctors put in me. I remember my first injections of Largactyl—too much dosage. To me, that was a prehistoric beast lumbering through me. I rate it as not a clean drug. It hit me like a train and left its mark of side effects. Who put the dehydrator in my mouth? Will someone please pick me up off the floor? Yet for some people this would be the drug of choice—it is clean and works great for them.

Finding the right drug can be trial and error and requires patience. I remember the first anti-depressant I was on. The doctor told me it could take a few tries to find the right one. My previous depth of suicidal depression always lasted two to three months. The drug would take a month to start to work. You do the math. I would only have a couple of tries at it.

I remember the buildup of anti-depressant in my system—a nervous spirit of energy grew in my spine and wanted to escape from my limbs, especially my legs. It was worse at night when trying to sleep—all I could do was to shake my legs. It helped a bit but the surge would build again. I weighed the cost as being worthwhile if it would take the bottom from my suicide major. I hated the hole of suicide meditation: all my time spent on how to do it, and putting it off till the next day.

It was Zoloft and it did take the bottom of suffering away. It was a nice change and it did not send me high. It was around this time I gave up my major highs and stopped slipping to that depth of depression. I didn't need to take Zoloft the next year.

A toolkit has many tools and I believe that we as bipolar people need different drugs for different applications—though you may only need a mood stabilizer. Do you know yourself and your illness? This is the most important aspect of medications. Are you in touch with your situation? Have you communicated with your doctor to get him or her on the same page?

No one else is in your head and that is the arena of sport we play in: the gladiators are bloodthirsty. Your doctor is not in your head so you better communicate to her your state of mind. I know this is challenging: it is in our mind where this illness attacks us. Take it easy. In time you will get a handle on your situation. Be gentle and try to make a little progress. Next year will be better. This is an endurance sport.

Chances are in the beginning your doctor will see you at your extremes, and will treat you for your high and your low and if he knows that you fluctuate in your mood he will probably introduce a mood stabilizer. This is all good. I hope that your medication works great for you. Remember it is there to work for you. Co-operate with it and your doctor. Your doctor does not know exactly what is going on with you, though doctors can read much from your speech, mannerisms, and interactions.

But if you are anything like me, one big thing that bipolar creates is the ability to act, to present a different experience outwardly than what is happening internally. It is a survival mechanism—it is a good thing. Yet it can be a horrible thing if you are never aware of it and it takes you for a long ride of deceit all the way to your death. To be real is a great and worthwhile pursuit.

What is your attitude toward drugs? Are they still recreational? Are they strictly for good? Have you ever self-medicated? Congratulations, I think it is a great trait to want to straighten yourself out. Your brain chemicals do not work properly and you need intervention. You have help now and are on your road to recovery, you have a doctor and you have medicine to help you. You have medications designed to assist your brain to work better. Alcohol and cocaine are not designed to help your mental illness, and they will mess with your dopamine and serotonin levels.

You are you; you are different from me, with unique issues. I went through detox and rehab when I was twenty. Addiction issues are common with bipolar. I stress that self-medicating can be a great thing: you want to repair yourself. We need to embrace that spirit and use it to balance your challenge.

Your doctor needs to know about your particular personality with drugs. You have to kill your addictive self and rise like the phoenix and use addictive drugs again for your best interest. It is messed up. You have to graduate from Narcotics Anonymous or Alcoholics Anonymous or Cocaine Anonymous and then throw out their big books. You have to forge through your wilderness and blaze your own trail through the dark. You can use their principles but you will have to ignore some of their advice as well. You need this drug like your very air.

An integral tool in my toolkit is a guard to slap my face to sleep. If I lose one full night's sleep I have to throw the cover on and get sleep or I am flying higher, and the higher I go, the harder it is to come down. Momentum builds. If I catch my loss of sleep in the early stages I prevent my mania. I prevent months of insanity and depression by taking a sleeping medication, or an anti-psychotic that promotes sleep when my thoughts are not of this world.

I approach sleep with natural tools such as chamomile tea, Calms, Rescue Remedy, and limit my caffeine in the later part of the day. I exercise and have sex. I take a hot bath and relax with slow music and a candle—I have read that when the body cools down it tends to go to sleep. Sometimes listening to white noise helps me; I like FM static on low. Sometimes earplugs help me. But there comes the point, less often if my lifestyle is in balance, when I have to take a pill for sleep.

If you struggle with sleep all the time, you'd better be an expert on sleep. Please take an interest in all approaches to a problem—medication is the big solution. If you use many little methods to guard your sleep, they may build to give you a great night's rest. And you won't have to bring out the big solution as much.

Some sleeping medications have more stone-over, or half-life than others. One will give you less than others; should you be driving in the morning on that stone-over? I have always found great results in reducing the dose. Talk to your doctor—half of a sleeping pill might just do it for you and produce less need for coffee or tea in the morning.

I have found that certain sleeping pills are not good for regular use: I was on one that was all right for occasional use but when I used it several days in a row, it stole my ability for R.E.M. sleep, and my brain was not fully rested. You could take the same drug and have different effects. Talk to your doctor. Just using sleeping medication can promote beneficial highs, yet we run the risk of raging psychosis or crashing into depression. It is better for me to use a sleep promoting anti-psychotic that slows my misfiring synapses.

It depends on your illness patterns as to what medications you need. You will need to build trust with your doctor to build your toolkit. No overdoses and then calling 911! Please call the crisis line and your support network before and instead of overdosing. Your doctor will have to trust you that you will not abuse your drugs on hand. It can take years to return to this point after abuse.

Be easy on yourself. Remember that the enemy strikes us in our thinking and it is there that you have to get it together and build your castle to live in. You are in that head and heart of yours. Hello in there. You can do it. Build your support network to lean on.

For those in psychosis, suicidal depression, and mixed states—you will be in contact with your doctor. You are most likely a danger to yourself and others. Remember to take these three places seriously: suicidal depression, manic psychosis and the mix of the two—consult your professionals. You need and deserve help.

The toolkit is meant more for preventing your highs and your lows. After you live with the creature of bipolar for several years or cycles you will get to know its ways and patterns. I have experienced the full spectrum: it was a predictable yearly cycle that required a different medication treatment in each season. My occasional need now is to have an anti-psychotic to guard my sleep that slows, and cleans up my thoughts. I require more of it with an increased stress level.

I found that my manic highs became more violent to myself as time went on. It became vital to my life to medicate the manic monster to death while it still ran, before it flew.

There is a spectrum in tranquilizers, at the one end they knock you out, sedate you; and at the other end they clean up your thoughts, and remedy psychosis. And you can get tranquilizers that are in between with a mix of both effects. Talk to your doctor and discover what is best for you. If you feel yourself slipping to manic and you do not have something to bring you down, get to your doctor now. And maybe for next time she will trust you to have something on hand, because you have been mature and you know your needs.

There was a level of mania for me that required injections of tranquilizer. I found that oral medication did not cover me enough. The injections became a safety blanket for me—I was comforted that I would not do anything crazier and hurt myself further. They brought me back into focus and calmed my frenetic mind.

After raging high for days with no sleep, I loved my first injections. They set me free, I could lie down and stretch, everything was beautiful. I was sedate, steady, and on my way back from the scary corners of psychosis. I loved aspects of psychosis and mania, yet it always turned on me, to horrific consequences, and threatened my life.

Certain medications require another medication to counter its side effects. If you are on a tranquilizer that causes side effects that require a side-effect medication, you will want to take it. I did not have enough Cogentin once and will never forget the discomfort.

Some of our medication can have a recreational side to it. As long as the medicinal outweighs the recreational and the recreational is not why you are taking it. Please do not misunderstand me—I am not advocating recreational use of your drugs. If you have to take them for medicinal reasons, please enjoy what they have to offer and make the best of it. It will help the drug work better if you believe in it.

You have to be responsible for your illness and your medications. You are as responsible as your doctor is to find the dosages and drugs that work for you. Be aware of the adjustments required as your life changes. My needs for medication have changed drastically over the years. My doctor and I have to stay on top of it.

My present toolkit includes a sleeping pill, and a major tranquilizer for preventative when my thoughts start to wander those psychotic hallways. You will come to know. We will talk later about psychosis. In my rough days I had an oral tranquilizer that was middle of the road between sedating and cleaning up thoughts. On my slip upwards I would guard my sleep and take the oral when I needed it for psychotic thoughts. If I came back down, fine; in my more stable days I would make note of it and not see my doctor till my next appointment.

Your doctor is not with you twenty-four hours per day. What we are striving for here is freedom through interdependence. You are you living the best you can with an illness that can kill you. Talk to your doctor and plan the attacking of your highs and lows, and whatever else you need to deal with.

In my experience the sooner I caught a high or low, I lessened the severity and the later rebound effect to the other extreme. I did not lose as much time regaining my right mind.

Developing a reliable tool kit can take a decade for some people: it can take longer or shorter. It depends on many factors. It depends greatly on you and your ability to face your addictions, and your ability to be honest. Do you truthfully want to move on in this illness to your gift? Are you making lifestyle changes that make you a more balanced person?

I believe that many people want to be ill. Our society lacks community and warmth and purpose. Illness can be a perverse friend. It can be a badge of honor. It can be many things: a co-dependent thing, a means to repel or get back at people. I for one decided that I had no need for someone to feel sorry for me. I desired to turn this thing into positive. Sure I have bipolar, I make the best of it.

Unfortunately my many attempts at using mood stabilizers did not help me. Your toolkit will hopefully have your middle of your road staple—it could be your regular doses of whatever you take as a mood stabilizer. Maybe you take the same thing year round, for years, and it works great for you, and you need nothing else. Congratulations!

Medications have purpose to make you better. They can also mess you up. Do your homework and understand your needs and how the drugs work. This bipolar would be an easier illness to live with if it was always the same: it would be easier to treat with the same drug.

Some of you can strive to be in the equator of mood and will never wander up or down to any negative consequence. Give thanks. I hope you can get down to the minimal medication that assists you. Some of us are able to go off all medication later in life—this can take years and much work to taper down. And others need to increase their medication as they get older.

Every one of us is different and is affected by each drug in our own way. Once again you have to be strict with yourself to know each bright and dark corner of this topic. Don't give up; it took me years to get a good handle on it. I had to struggle to get away from an over-medicating doctor. He believed he had to put the chemical straight jacket on his patients. That did not mean that I had to stay under his care to my grave.

As people who need medications it leaves us in a difficult spot if a person of authority feels that they have a right, and it is good, to overdose you. When you are on too much of one thing, you may need more of something else to counter the effects of the first one—it can snowball on you.

For me, over-medication was a big part of my disability with the illness. It was my responsibility to deal with this. It took time and I needed an enlightened doctor. I worked with my doctor to find the right dosage and drug and threw many to the wayside. It takes practice to find what works best.

How are your pharmaceutical stocks performing? It is a shame that profit is linked to something useful, yet easily exploited. Should lunches be bought, for medical personnel, by pharmaceutical representatives? Should our medical personnel choose a certain medication because of the salesperson giveaways?

How do your family views on medications, affect you? I had family members who frowned on my use of medication. Later they developed a medical condition and now they have accepted their medications as needed. I am on much less medication now and they do not strive to change their lifestyles to require less medication. People and family can be challenging: you have your own stories.

In my days of attending Narcotics Anonymous, the people who surprised me most were the older ladies that tended to be the prescription drug addicts. They faced a medically-encouraged addiction. When I was in detox there was a man who had been on Valium for longer than I had been alive. He was coming off of it and his limbs shook; his hands moved close to two feet when I first met him. How is a doctor allowed to do that to someone?

Years ago I tried the drug Ativan in my time of tendency to fly manic. That is one smooth drug—which deserves its reputation for being addictive. It is rated as anti-anxiety: for some reason it caused anxiety attacks with me and I had to get off it. It worked for a while and then it turned on me. I had never experienced panic attacks before. They were terrible and I hope to never go through them again. And for some of you, Ativan is perfect. We are complex, unique individuals.

What medications do you need and what works for you? Be careful and diligent in your pursuit of the right drug and dosage. It can change.

Medication is a tricky subject with concerns: addictions, side effects, cost, and over-medication. The drugs can steal your personality and your ability to read or talk. You might have gained a hundred pounds. You might not be able to move and have a sore buttock. Relax when you receive your injection—breathe and find a happy place and tell the nurse to wait till you are relaxed; it can make a big difference.

But we need medication desperately. Make the best of them. It is great if you have other forms of healing, give thanks. Many approaches add up to a greater foundation. Please remember that the drugs are there to help you help yourself. Cooperate with your doctor and communicate. My tool kit helped me regain my life. I hope that you can do the same with yours.

Points of thought and action:

#1 Have I accepted my need for medication?

#2 Why do I need medication? Make a file and understand my drug information from my pharmacist.

#3 What does each medication do for me, and why do I need it in my toolkit?

#4 Do I need different dosages and medications? (Talk to my doctor.)

#5   How am I dealing with any addiction concerns I have?
#6   (My personal plan.)

OVER THE DOSE

We all have our reasons for overdose phenomenon. I used Lithium once to try to counter my rising tide of mania. It wasn't a classical overdose in the sense that I took a few at a time and then took more with the intent to remedy my slide to the highs of mania. It was not a suicide. My doctor had not empowered me to eliminate my highs. I was doing the best with what I had on hand.

I have second hand experience observing repeat overdosing—they were driven. The one would take the bottle of sleeping pills and then call 911—did he want to really kill himself or was it a cry for help? It could very well have been some issues to do with his parents—he was getting their attention.

We are each unique with our reasons. But we have all lost hope and felt we have no reason to live. I suggest that you read the *Hope and Suicide* chapter closely and make your hope chest and list of things to do in case of suicidal thinking.

Overdosing can be a form of self-medicating. We have not received the proper medications to counter the illness and we have to try more quantity to hit the spot that needs hitting. We need to talk to our doctor and find the correct medications for our bodies and minds. It is our responsibility.

We have to face our internal demons, we have to forge through the negative of our lives and we have to forgive and forget and simply move on into our new lives. It is much easier to say than live. A friend told me the other day that she leaves it in the past and moves on. It does her no good to keep looking back—she has learned all she can and has to face forward.

Overdosing comes down to responsibility for your life and your issues and it plays out in medication. It is not only a problem with medication—underlying reasons trigger. It can be your doctor and your relationship with him. It could be lack of responsibility and desire to get better. Are you holding onto your illness to stroke your old self—do people respond to you only in dramatics and chaos? Are you afraid of success? Do you deserve good in your life? Our lives can be set up in strange ways for love and acceptance.

We need to be aware of how overdosing is triggered and to catch it in the initial stages. If you recognize patterns with your counselors, you need to write a plan of attack that when you reach for the bottle, perhaps a little card will be attached to your bottle of pills. The card gives you simple steps to follow: call this person, call the crisis line. It could be to take one pill and flush the rest immediately.

You can get more medication. Maybe you only get one or two or three days supply at a time. You can gain more trust and responsibility in time. The most important thing is to keep you alive and grow hope and a reason to live and to narrow your extremes and dramatics to a balance so you can approach your gift. It waits for you and you will never fully appreciate your gift until you leave this misuse of medications.

Get medications that work and learn to use them properly with your doctor. It is a key to our wellness. Your doctor could promote your misuse of medications by giving you the wrong ones. Communicate with your doctor and find the right ones. Take some steps away from illness and misuse of drugs. It is your responsibility and your right—if you are faithful in the small uses of medication, you will be trusted and empowered to take big steps into a life you did not think was possible. It waits there for you now.

Walk toward the gift and open it. We need medications to minimize the illness. Some of us get to the point of zero pharmaceuticals and this is great. Many of us have to take a lot of medication before we get settled and balanced with this bipolar. Many of us will be on medication for life. The longer we screw around before settling down into our maintenance dosages, the more medications we will have to be exposed to, not to mention their screwing with our chemistry.

We have many issues to deal with involving medication. Overdosing has roots in your internal world and your past; have you resolved your past and how it affects you? It will haunt you in many ways and make your life miserable. You need to minimize and prioritize how you will react to your past. It is your life and you can choose to move on and forgive and forget and take on new clothes and thinking and feeling. Sometimes we have to leave the past in the past—there is no other way.

And if we have attempted overdoses we need to nurture our deep gardens of self. We did terrible things to our bodies and minds and we need to sow seeds of peace and forgiveness. We have to embrace the spirituality of hope and peace and love to remedy this dark place. We can post lights to guide ourselves through these dark corners of our soul. The more times that we go down a path in our minds, the more of a hard-wired road it will be. It is very challenging to not go down those same roads again: for our entire lives it may come up from time to time as an easy, appropriate solution. We absolutely need to rewire our thinking to not go to these places of destruction. Let the weeds and trees grow up to block the road and detour your thinking into highways that lead to oasis.

The light of forgiveness can shine in these closets—we are not the only ones to have done this. Shame can shrivel and dry up, and we can lubricate fountains of joy and peace in its place. You can do it and you need to grieve for what you have done: cry and yell and feel the experience. Maybe grieving will teach you what you need to know to move on.

We can get stuck in cycles and modes that perpetuate themselves to no end. We need to approach the situation in a new way to break the cycle. Try fresh approaches and embrace and reward your responsibility and progress. Celebrate your new life. Have a party for a week without overdosing. Treat yourself for making it past your one year anniversary.

Your gift is waiting for you to live.

Points of thought and action:
#1   Have I overdosed?
#2   What are the true deep reasons why?
#3   How do I prevent it from reoccurring?
#4   How do I feel and grieve the experience of over-dosing?
#5   How do I forgive myself and move on?
#6   (My personal plan.)

SEX

Our sex drive is affected by the illness. It can increase or decrease. It can cause us to act sexually like we would never act in our right mind. Bipolar can take away all inhibitions—this makes it exciting and dangerous.

When I was depressed my sexual drive decreased—it is one of the few times when my drive is virtually suspended. When I had no significant other, there was no possibility of hooking up with a partner in my depression. Since I have been married I have not slipped to the depths of depression but even at the beginning stages for me I do not want sex.

It can be hard on our loved ones to understand that it is not them. We need to educate them and ourselves on the effects of the illness in all areas of life including sex. We need to communicate to our partner concerning our lack of libido. It can be a symptom of the lack in our lifestyle. We may not be sleeping enough or eating properly or exercising or our self-esteem is wrecked from our episodes.

We can recognize the sexual patterns in our illness. Write it down on your daily calendar—it can be a confirming factor of where you are and a predicting factor of where you will be.

We are unique sexual beings and bipolar will change your sexual patterns. How has it affected you thus far? We need to be gentle with ourselves regarding our changing sexuality.

Our loved ones can be patient and assist us. And it is up to us to deal with it. Maybe we need to help them please themselves just by laying beside them—we need to touch them, we need to get over the idea of intimacy being intercourse alone; there are many forms of showing love. Explore your options.

Loved ones can help you live the right lifestyle choices for you—they might go for a walk with you and enjoy holding hands. With bipolar we can lose touch with ourselves and it may help to be reminded of your great attributes—why do they love you? What do they like about you?

We can and should write down positive traits and aspects of ourselves when we are lucid, we can refer to these when we need a boost. This bipolar can tear us into numbness.

The greatest change that bipolar may induce in you is turning you into a sexual extrovert open to encounters that you would not usually have. Hypo and mania changes us to lose touch with our morals and self-protecting ideals. In the world of sexually transmitted diseases and A.I.D.S. it is not a great thing to be running around having unprotected sex with strangers. And when we are manic, people are more open to us and we can be more desirable—therefore we can have more experiences.

This is another tough subject to overcome. You have been depressed and on medication that has taken away all sexual desire for many months—you slip up into hypo and you find yourself turned on by a total stranger and you flirt with her. She flirts back and you are suddenly advancing to clothes off and you don't even know her and her potential diseases. It can happen fast.

I have had regrets over manic encounters—my manic head was on autopilot. I was like a teen unaware of any danger. I had a woman tell me at the last minute about her genital herpes. I stopped and am thankful that I had the lucidity to walk away. I hadn't touched her vagina area but I was still scared and called the S.T.D. Line. It was an interesting conversation.

If I had been in my full mind these events would not have transpired the way they did. We can be out of touch with who we are and not care about consequences.

There is no denying the increase of libido in me as I entered hypo and mania. I am a horny beast that needs sex. I met a guy that slept with many, many women and wrote about his escapades and killed himself. Did he have regrets? We can all have certain regrets but which ones are you willing to carry with you? Would getting a sexually transmitted disease and transmitting it to twenty people be enough for you to kill yourself, if you were down and depressed? For some it is more than enough.

As bipolar people we need to explore what we want sexually. In our times of right mind we need to take responsibility for our sexual lives. Do you ever want to settle down and be content with one partner? You may decrease your chances of ability to be content if you sleep with hundreds of people. If that is what you want, go for it. Be aware of what you are doing. Protect yourself and others.

We are unique. Some bipolar people have experimented with sexual acts and homosexual and lesbian sex and they will never be the same. They struggle with the memories of what they did and have a tendency to keep opening the doors for excitement. If this is you, I wish you contentment and a happy sex life. Choose what you want to live with. Do you want those situations in your head for all time? Accept yourself for who you truly are. If you need to, forgive yourself and move on.

I am thankful that I was closed off sexually and afraid to open my hyper sexuality stage. I was a late bloomer and then an introvert—I didn't make it too far sexually and I am fine with that, things worked out great.

When I became hypo and manic, I became a sexual creature. I flirted and women responded. Something had changed—I was sexual and capable of many partners. I wanted the love act to mean something and waited for the love to happen. The greatest thing I found to protect me was to masturbate. It was, and is, great to get release of those energies. The release only does so much, but it has put me to sleep on many occasions. I have a lover now and I still masturbate on occasion. We can't have sex all the time and it is part of my lifestyle that helps me live with the surges of energy. It has saved me from sexual acts with women I care nothing about.

Morals come into this picture of sex and I believe that this is a great thing. Are you aware of your morals and what you want to live with in memories? Having morals is not a bad thing, to be afraid of, nor is it a reason to place yourself above others. I did not want to have fifty lovers before I settled down to marriage. Nor did I want to be a virgin. We should not judge one another for these choices. We need to be aware that these are choices and each carries with it a set of pluses and minuses, as well as responsibilities.

In this day and age, if you have binges of sexual activity, I hope and trust that you protect yourself and others. The best protection from sexual diseases is abstinence. Condoms only do so much. Awareness and education are keys. If you are going to be sexually active learn what you need to know. If you get a Sexually Transmitted Disease, it can have effects for life. It can take your life—can you accept that?

When I prepared for my Cuba trip I packed a box of condoms. It is not the end-all of protection but it helped me approach the situation. I wanted some sexual action, but I also wanted to beat the mania. Which one should be my priority? I had to be ready to counter and eliminate both if needed. Sex can be wonderful and love can be amazing. They can be great distractions and diversions—they can be the main event. My living the gift of bipolar superseded my need for sex.

I stepped off the plane and flew high—I was horny and women were receptive. Prostitutes were everywhere but I did not want to open that door. An attractive Canadian offered her interest anytime—she was sexy and I wanted her. My illness flared up and took priority. I had to deal with it. Perhaps, by holding onto my sexual energy, it contributed to my psychosis.

I ended up having an innocent romance with another Canadian. It was sweet and only went to holding hands and kissing and caressing. It was what I needed to heal and stay steady in balance. I did not need a sex beast to rock my world—my world was upside down as it was.

Our sexual power as bipolar people is a key to the gift. Sex sells products and services. Sex is the power of sales and the energy to produce. There is strength in feeling sexy and horny and then channeling this energy into your actions; whether it is in business or pleasure. It is your powerful ally, but it can turn on you and steal all the good that you have. It can wreck your marriage through an affair. You need to be aware of its power and volatility. Take control.

Think and Grow Rich (reference #4) has a chapter on sex transmutation. It is basically channeling your sexual energy into productive pursuits other than sex. The subject may creep you out, but be aware of how it affects you. If you have mania that has a high sexual energy to it, you'd better get a handle on it before it takes you apart. I tend to get horny and I funnel that energy into my writing before I seek sexual intimacy—my writing is better because of this.

The other night I was out with friends to see a blues act. It was electrical, intense blues and it was sensual. The dance floor was full. I watched women tractor-beamed to the lead singer-guitar player—they were after the bad boy image and there was no mistaking the sexual energy in the air. Women stared and swayed and twisted: he sucked it in and glared right back at them and made love to them with his guitar and voice. Women danced with him alone that night: his guitar playing and voice sounded a step above for this reason. Is this why live music most always sounds better?

Salespeople and the entertainment industry use sexual energy to market their products all the time. The movie stars thrive on this. Rock stars glory in it. What can it do for you? Can it develop your abilities and make money for you so that you can live your live in a healthier way?

People respond well to me in person and this is partially due to the manic sexual energy that I have. I strive to make this a good thing and not evil or dirty. It is a fact of life. A nice smile exchanged can be a light form of this. People who are sexual are successful in what they pursue. They have energy and the drive to go after their dreams.

We need to be easy on ourselves with our changing libidos and to be honest and open with our partners. We need to forgive ourselves and move on from our regrettable escapades. We need to be aware of the hyper-sexuality that can be part of our mania. We need to somehow set standards for our sexual partners that we can live with.

Alcoholics Anonymous has a recommendation that when you first straighten out you should not be romantically involved for a year. This can be easier on your head while you sort through your illness to the gift that is yours. But a significant other can also greatly assist you in this process of living your gift. If you have someone good, hold onto that person and flourish in your relationship. But if you are single now, don't complicate your existence until you get a better handle on your life. Masturbation can protect us physically, emotionally, and mentally from bad relationships. Masturbation can also develop into an addiction—we have to guard against the negatives of it.

I strove to deal with the baggage in my life before seeking a significant other. I am extremely glad that I focused on being single and getting through my negative and leaving the illness behind. It has made me more steady on my own, and ultimately a better husband. My marriage completes me and is not a co-dependency thing. The great thing was that my wife was out there also working at being single and sorting through the negative in her life. There could be someone out there waiting for you. They are getting their life together for you, are you getting it together for them? It may be part of your gift.

I know someone who lives the gay man lifestyle. He desperately wants someone to love and be loved by. He has told me the extreme approach to sex—for many it is the eternal never content consumption of sexual partners. This is a good description of opening fully to the sex that mania can offer you.

How many partners are enough? I am not saying that you will be gay. I don't care about your sexual preferences. I only care that you are aware of the power you possess to change your life for good and bad. How do you want to live? Do you want to be a sexual addict? Mania can wedge that door open.

I believe our greatest problem in relationships is the inability we have to live as single people and deal with the negatives in our lives. It is fascinating and sad how a daughter of an alcoholic father grows up. If she doesn't deal with the alcoholism: she will be attracted to an addict or alcoholic. When will we as a society deal with this in childhood?

A father sexually abuses his daughter and son. Neither of them deals with it and grows up. The son abuses his own children and the daughter hooks up with an abuser and enables his abuse of her children. These are generalizations that have exceptions. The point is we have to deal with our problems before we hook up with someone—if we do not deal with it, the person we will be attracted to will be part formula problem from our past. Are you aware of your past and your family and how it affects you?

Sex is a wonderful gift and I hope that you can enjoy it. Sex can be the icing on a loving relationship. Have fun with it and be aware of its power and channel the energy. It is dangerous and can drive us into, and keep us in, the wrong relationships that can ruin our lives. Don't be afraid to masturbate—it can save you from a lot of pain. Don't be ashamed of it. The world would be a better place if it were practiced more.

Bipolar can give us great sexual power to channel into our creations and lives. I hope that you have the strength and courage to live your life single and get your life together and then find the woman or man of your dreams. It will still be hard work but the major work on yourself and your past will be done. It gets easier. You can do it. Don't accept a partner who is wrong for you. And if you are with the right person now and it works, celebrate.

Revel in the gift of sexual energy.

Points of thought and action:

#1 How has bipolar affected my sex life?

#2 What is dangerous about bipolar sex?

#3 What are my tendencies with sex?

#4 How do I protect myself from harm?

#5 How can I channel my sexual energy into other areas of my life for good?

#6 (My personal plan.)

RELATIONSHIPS

Sex comes before relationships in this book because bipolar may cause it to be in that order. In the early stages with bipolar we may be in a relationship with someone because of sex and our desire for this person. This desire may be fleeting and temporary yet we find ourselves living with the person for months and years. We can make big decisions in a hurry, like moving in with someone.

With bipolar we can find ourselves waking up to an odd situation. We may lose our sanity and re-discover ourselves as different persons doing unusual things. This includes our new relationships. Part of us goes on holiday when we are taken over by the mentally ill side.

This negative bipolar side of us may be attracted to someone and initiate a relationship that our usual self would never be interested in. This can lead to awkward situations and more confusion for us when we are regaining our sanity. Again, if you are single it is ideal to remain single when you begin dealing with illness. You have enough other things to be concerned about.

Sure there are exceptions, and I wish you the best if you are in a relationship that you found in your illness stages. Perhaps the two of you are ill. It can provide great encouragement, understanding, and camaraderie to be together. It can be a great boost, and edifying for the two of you.

Sometimes you can bring each other down: I observed a bipolar couple and one of them always seemed to be in a crises of hospitalization from being up or down. There were always dramatics and chaos. I think they were happy at times but from the outside it looked like they reacted to the chaos in the other. It was a continual bizarre lack of peace. I did not observe them leaving illness or approaching their gift stage.

Perhaps if they could have searched out some space from each other, they could have each climbed a few rungs of health and together they could have stopped mirroring the illness. They could have got back together. Most of us would agree that it is a better quality of life to not experience the extremes of bipolar, that they are dangerous places to visit or dwell in. Does your relationship hold you toward balance or illness?

It is up to each of us to choose our relationships and make the best of them. Is it the best time for you to be involved with someone? When I was involved in my ill days I ran the risk of getting better and them not getting better. I have tried to be a caregiver in mental health and found that it had merit but I did not want to go there long term—it wears me down. I do not need a significant other that I have to look after. I needed someone that has understanding or experience with mental illness but does not suffer with it. Are you conscious of your power in deciding who you go out with? This one decision has great effect for our future good and bad.

I wanted to be the best I could be before hooking up with someone. Part of this is selfish. I deserve the best partner because I have worked hard to eliminate the negative from my life. I am aware of how someone can bring me down and I do not want to go there.

If I hooked up with a woman in the midst of my illness—when my quality of life was poor—then my life would be doubly challenged. I would tend to get stuck there. I tended to attract women around my own level of functioning. I had to learn to get rid of women I had attracted in my times of trouble. I had nothing against them but I had to be honest and not be with someone that was wrong. It can be difficult to be true to yourself and to leave someone who provides comfort and enjoyment. Struggling to stay single and become healthier can be the best thing we can do for our future ability to be in relation with a significant other.

Do you know anyone who remains with the wrong person and is afraid and unable to let them go? I know several. I believe this is one of the major reasons why we are not happy in marriages and relationships. We are not taught to be successful singles first—we need to get our lives together and be true to ourselves and know what we need and want. Then we can have the dignity and awareness to not fall into love with our dad or mom's influence. There are patterns of attraction that affect our every move in relationships—do you know how you are influenced? Are you a fortunate one who is free and clear to operate on your own? If so, your parents were relationally healthy and passed on good abilities—that is great.

We all tend to be influenced in some way by our upbringing. You can tarnish your entire life by going along with these influences. Three children with someone you picked because he or she was like your parent—you get your life together and realize that you have to leave that person to help your kids and yourself. Good for you. We jump into relationships too lightly. We have the fairy tale desires of Hollywood and TV, but our reality can be very different. How does bipolar affect your ability to have a meaningful relationship?

In the short run, bipolar took away my ability to have anything of significance with women. It upset me at the time and I took it as a negative thing. I was messed up and only capable of attracting dramatics and strife that further taxed my head. What I did not realize was that it was protecting me—it allowed me time to heal. It left me with a cleaner slate to deal with—I did not have relationship confusion to deal with, though in my times of psychosis I brought up past relationships. It would be tough to be in a relationship and go through psychosis.

Your situation is yours. You may have met someone in the hospital and you are both growing in health and happiness—good for you. Please be conscious of your relationship decisions.

I had one ex that was much better than me in many ways—her family did not experience any mental health issues and had trouble with me. I was not aware of the gift side yet and they did not see anything positive in me for their lovely daughter. They wanted the best for their loved one. At the time it upset me but I am glad in the long run. It was a complicated attraction that was difficult to end—it surged in unhealthy cycles.

We should talk a bit about in-laws and stigma. Your significant other is attracted to you for many reasons and hopefully you are plugged into the gift side of bipolar. Your mother-in-law judges you and your fiancé accepts you for being bipolar: can your fiancé defend you and set the stigmatizing person straight?

This can be a test of whether you should be involved with him or her. If this person doesn't deal with mom or dad and their stigma issues perhaps this person is not for you. Your significant other should be there for you and you for them—you should protect and cherish each other. On some occasions your significant other could be subconsciously using you to get back at parents who do not want a mentally ill person as their son or daughter's spouse. It can be an intricate world out there.

Be wary before you commit to serious steps. You and I both want to believe in the perfection of love above all else. We can believe it for as long as we want but life has its way of barging in.

"Your mother said I'm crazy."

"You are crazy."

"You promised not to say that again."

It is up to you to live your life to enhance it with your significant other. You can wreck your life and have a tough time to remedy it with the wrong person. We need to take responsibility for our love lives.

This can be a messy situation that can grow to serious consequences and it can cause you to focus on the negative side of bipolar. Depending on how close an interaction you need to have with the in-law stigmatic—perhaps you see them every three years—it is better left alone. It can be a character flaw in them—they would be unhappy with anyone their child chooses to be with. They themselves are unhappy and will sabotage their own child's happiness. There are many situations out there. What is yours?

Are you displaying only your illness traits or does your true great personality shine through with the gift side of bipolar? For some people it is simple ignorance on their part. They hear the words mental illness and they panic and judge. I find that some of these people are not healthy themselves. Certain people are stuck in their ways of ignorance. Nothing you can do will change their state of mind. Maybe, in time, they will change their opinion about you.

Perhaps we can blame our lack of positive media attention for this in-law stigma. This could be part of our solution, to be plugged into our gift sides and educate our world on the greatness of bipolar. Do people judge their loved one's fiancé for suddenly being stricken with a physical illness? Usually not.

It can be a messed up world when our parents decide whether significant others are fit for us. Some of this can be leftover from historical survival times. It is understandable that they want the best for us: we should want the best for us. Some parents like tall people, some like rich, or professionals. You could be any one of these traits and be horrible and that would be fine.

It ultimately comes down to you and yours wanting each other and a life together; yet you need to be aware of how a family member can put a wedge between you and your significant other. It may come down to distancing yourself from family if they are ignorant toward bipolar. And not every person is able to put his or her spouse before the family. I believe you leave your family to start a new one—sure, you still have ties but ultimately you are moving onto a new branch.

In today's world of moving around it seems that family is changing all the time. I moved away from where my family lives and I find I need to adopt new family members. My family is always my family but my new adopted family can be healthier and more satisfying in certain ways. Our families can be stuck in spots and unable to move on—we can still love them and interact and we can accept new people into our lives. It can be very healthy and good for us. Community and belonging are strong frameworks for us to reduce the illness and live in the gift.

It is easy for me to spout off and say this yet I still have issues in my life—some of the most frustrating of them involving family. We cannot choose our families. I can choose how I deal with my life and bipolar and grow and change; but my family might not grow or change or my in-laws might have their own set of problems. I can change only my life for certain. The most control I have with family is how I react to them.

Family members sometimes react to the way we were: they have not had bipolar mould them into different people, and they do not understand who we have become. A relationship can be stuck in the past, but one of the parties has changed. We have to update into the present. The important thing is to be empowered to choose and develop health and happiness in your relationships— and let go of certain things that will never change. Some people never change and have a hard time respecting change in others.

Some families want to keep you down—then you are predictable. Everyone is stricken and safe in unhappiness, chaos reigns. We all come from different family situations and our significant other is from another. How can you stick together and control how much energy you focus on family? My wife and I have to monitor certain frustrations to do with our families—it does no good to dwell on them. Acceptance is a key to peace. Facing certain problems and accepting your part in them is important: between the first draft and the polished version of this book we have made major strides.

Bipolar can be the worst and the best of times. I am sometimes a hard person to be married to. If I was still controlled by the illness side it would be brutal to be married to me. I am thankful that I am not predominately in illness anymore, and that I didn't hook up with someone then. We must focus and grow the best in ourselves. I love big, my priorities include my wife; I am sensitive and know myself.

Sometimes timing is crucial. I believe I was not capable of a successful relationship until I had my life together. I lived in balance and was able to bring some of my best to the table. I could communicate and live for someone else, I could compromise. I wish that you could strive to be happy and healthy in singleness first and foremost. This may help you to leave your illness side and move toward your gift. When you do find a great partner it may work as a catapult to launch you fully to leave your illness and go into your gift.

And if you have a great partner now, revel in that person and make the best of your relationship. What I love about being with someone is that one of us is usually positive in attitude—we can feed our attitude of joy and peace and goodness. The other is able to support when one of us occasionally struggles.

We are the creators of our attitude and this involves your significant other-created life. You have the power to choose love and joy and contentment in spite of the circumstances. What will really matter about today ten or twenty years from now?

Build each other up and make a great life for yourselves—strive to enjoy everyday.

Points of thought and action:
#1   How does bipolar affect my present relationship?
#2   How does my present relationship affect my bipolar?
#3   How am I still affected relationally by my parents?
#4   If I am alone, can I stay that way and improve my life before a relationship?
#5   How can I change to better my relationship?
#6   (My personal plan.)

PEACE OVER FEAR

Bipolar can lead us down paths that promise wonders, then all turns to fear: all-consuming, paralyzing fear. Fear so terrible that it needs new words to describe it. Terror is a more appropriate word for the experiences.

Terror is a dangerous adversary that we need to take seriously. It can control and take us to the edge of our limits. Both extremes of bipolar, the manic psychosis and the suicidal depression, held terror experiences for me.

My fear in depression could be described as a basement that could not be escaped from—it lingered in my bones and sinew. I ached with fear in my meditations of gray. It felt like I could never escape this place of inflated realities of negative. I could not step out of my experience to get a fresh perspective on my life. From the dark depths of me, the fear of bad held me in place. I had no energy to talk to people, and no desire to reach out. I covered myself in the cycles of gloom thought.

These downward spirals always took me to a place where ending my life was an optimistic solution to end the suffering. Deep in my brain, my thoughts slowed to muddy tracks that fed upon themselves and capitulated. There was no known escape for me except to sleep and perhaps I could travel from my suffering into dreamland. My twisted dreams soothed my existence by getting my thoughts out of their continual domination.

I could not even motivate myself to move, I had to wait for weeks, it seemed like an eternity. I told myself this, too, will pass and there will be a brighter day—but when? I tried to look after myself and sometimes I was able to. At other times there was nothing that could be done.

Medication helped, and simple rest and a little food. I would eventually hit bottom and turn around. My absence of energy worked in my favor to keep me from acting on my suicidal constant—it did not come in urges for me in my deep depressions. It was more like a devotion, a constant meditation on how I could end my fear and suffering.

I would try to install new positive input over my dull aches of black thought. In the end I found it easier to learn to prevent my highs and change my actions to have less to regret. I then had fewer items to feel terrible about to taunt and beat myself with emotionally. I reduced the heights of my highs and therefore reduced the bounce back effect. The higher I flew, the lower I sunk to recover. I believe this is an effect of our bodies wanting to regain homeostasis. This balance is vital and the body will perform scary, wondrous feats to gain our balance. Like simply shutting down and refusing to carry us any further in these manic directions of flurry and change, and, then dumping us into recovery depression.

And part of how far I fell after a big manic psychosis was connected to the amount of medication that I was on. It is a tricky challenge to have enough medication to bring a manic down and then to taper off in time to reduce the descent into depression. I have found it easier to taper the amount on the mini highs than on the big highs. We can become huge forces of energy and we need thick dosage blankets to settle our high. Talk with your doctor about your experiences in this department. You may be able to give some insight about reducing your extremes and the momentum in which you react to the other extreme.

I keep thinking about the importance of seeking the middle of our experience: it is in the middle where we have the most lucidity to strengthen our ways for positive health. We have to wake ourselves up to the fact that when we feel that we are in touch with our true selves and personality, to remain there we need to work hard on shoring up these positive balanced places. We need to make decisions of what to do about placing controls over our slides into depression and our catapults into mania.

What makes us feel terrible in our depression? Stop doing these things. For me it tended to be weird things I did when I was manic. I had to stop going high, I had to come to a place where I wanted, I needed to give up my highs. I had to have a near-death accident to wake up to how serious this was. It would only spiral in power and danger. And this was not an overnight decision.

I did my back flip in the icy river, landed on my head and floated with the current. It took two to three days to get in the hospital. It took two to three months to be pain free in my shoulders and neck. It took two months to come down fully. I had a week of strong mixed states. I had a couple months of depression and suicidal dwelling. I had a couple months of climbing back out to a personality: is this me, really me?

This all takes time. I learned my lesson to give up my highs. I don't like these fearful places. It then took me close to a year to be in a steady state again. And after the months of depression, it is tempting to go high. It feels so wonderful to flow in those beginning stages, where everything looks brighter. Everything is enhanced. Smells smell better, my brain works perfectly, I can talk to anyone about anything.

This is all before the door slams and you are in a room with fear behind you and terror in front, not to mention what is above and below. Fear can manifest itself in a way that pushes you deeper into trouble. There is less negative to push further into the wilderness, alone. Who can walk beside us in these thoughts? Many of us do walk these horrific places, but how many are able to experience these places at the same time, to help us?

Maybe this could be part of our solution: many of us have been in similar suffering abysses. For me I was always alone in these lands. What if we could set up imaginary friends, guides that dwell in these places to help us feel secure in turning around before it gets too late? Imagine this guide helping you to look after yourself, to not go out naked into the snowy winter. Your imaginary guide and friend helps you on with your clothes and helps you to call your doctor and take your medication responsibly.

In writing this passage, the tears cloud my eyes. No one was in these places when I was stuck in them. The best technique is to prevent these extremes. But think for a moment; is it crazy to plant suggestions of imaginary helper guides to assist you in these lonely hellish places? Is it not mostly played out in our imaginations anyway? To journey in psychosis is beyond words.

Please prevent your dangerous extremes. Make decisions beforehand about how you will stop your manic spending (limit access to your funds and recognize crime is not an option.) Don't follow through with your sexual encounters (use masturbation.) Maybe you need to put yourself into a safe house of some sort with a relative or place limitation and visitations to and from your home. Prevent your extremes with medication and anything else that helps you.

And if you are like me and it takes years to remedy the extremes, build a case of multi-faceted tools to counter the dangers. Fear to me is a minor theme of psychosis. Terror is another step. There are no names for these next places. Normal people who have not experienced psychosis have no reference point to even consider the energy of psychosis. I think it could be beneficial in your right mind to think out a guide for yourself in times of emergency: plan it out to the point of what this guide looks like and how this guide talks and what the guide says. Use your prompt cards for this—leave some trail that will remind you of the existence of this imaginary, yet vital, ally in your wilderness of craze. Plant the seed for this helper to come to life in your imagination when you need him or her. Make it an angel if that works for you.

I will make one up too. Mine is nice and tender and helps with the pain, soothes the terror and allows me to rest and not obey the psychotic master. My angel takes the whips from the psychotic driver, and places me in a safe place and protects me from harm. Someone who will just hold me safe and allow me to feel something; to bring part of me back to this dimension. To allow me a taste of peace. I have depended on my belief in God in these states but it always took me further to a deserted dimension. I could be in crowds of people and in my suffering there was this state of utter aloneness.

I think that we are onto a tool here that can help us. Maybe you are a cat person and your madness guide would be a kitty that protected you and carried you back to a safe place where you did not have psychotic or suicidal thinking.

Some people in their right mind will have trouble to even see the need for this, let alone to construct this angel kitty in their minds. We are creative people who can create solutions for our dilemmas. We need to deal with the addictions we create, or have created for us through repetitive meditation on memories and emotions. I believe fear can also be an addiction. When I was giving up my highs, I discovered that I'd needed to watch horror flicks for this reason. It was a bit of a compulsion. I believe now that it was my addiction to fear and psychotic thinking and muted feeling. Now I do not like this sort of movie—I have severed my ties with these places and am moving into new ways of experience that I prefer: peace and joy and love.

I have had to forage new trail memories in my mind to not dwell on fear in my present and future life. By writing about a helper guide, I have found healing for my deepest horrific memories of being in solitary psychosis. I've cried a few tears and guided some of my hidden memories out of those deep dark places.

Can you fathom that we can be addicted to feelings? Even fear? Have you ever felt stuck in negative places and you just can't get out of the cycle? This is deep within your thinking and feeling focus.

Marinate you thoughts in positive words and passages and ideas. What you think of will grow. Do not watch the evening news before you go to bed. Turn the channel. The responsible thing to do, if you are sensitive, is to not expose yourself to the sufferings of others that you cannot help. Turn off the TV. Others want us to be addicted to the fear and knowing what evil lurks out there. Who cares? Live your life with those who you can help in a positive way. Your influence will bubble over into people. And the experience of people you influence in a positive way will spill over into other lives.

People speak of heaven and hell beginning on earth. I would agree that bipolar has soared me and dragged me through these experiences. Do not spoil your mind by getting caught up in the evils of the world. You will have illness by turning this negative focus into negative experience. Safeguard your mind and remove messages of fear from your experience. Plant new seeds of thoughts in place of judgments regarding the experience of bipolar. Think in new ways to grow your chosen feelings. Bipolar is a gift that is good. It is a challenge worth working through. I will work through it.

Input positive experiences of peace. Choose your input. Are you addicted to the who-done-it, cop or autopsy shows? When you are in the city do you ever think of what could go wrong in a criminal way? Is your thinking influenced by these shows' negative stories and images? We are subtle, sensitive and complex creatures. From deep within our minds spring our thoughts, actions and feelings. What seeds of fear have you planted in your subconscious mind?

Maybe you need to overcome that addiction and challenge your mind in a new positive way. Learn to overcome these conditioned cycles of memory and feeling. Replace your experience with positive input and you will change your life by changing your memories, thoughts and patterns of actions and feelings. Write positive affirmations for your new chosen life and read them out daily.

Perhaps if we just had the news media present positive community messages, we could change the patterns of the world. Older people are surprised by the acting out of young people. I am surprised that they are not worse than they are. There are amazing young people in the world. As adults we should be changing the experience that awaits the next generation. We have a choice to change our minds and our sphere of influence, and in that small way we will be changing our world and the world for future generations.

Deep seated pursuits of fear and greed drive parts of our world. Money is made through insurance over fear. Even when we buy our shiny new items, we're asked "Would you like an extended warranty with that?"

Horror movies are some of the cheapest to make and promise an assured return and profit. Many of our kids are addicted to the experience of being frightened. This has been going on for decades but the intensity has risen. For some of the horror trailers shown on TV, I have to close my eyes. Why do we let this escalate?

Is it the horror movie makers that are at fault? I think more so that it is our general society's focus on what can go wrong. Our habit of producing headline news with human suffering and selling advertising at the same time is sad. Making news programming is cheaper than many other programming options. Some channels have many hours of fear messages in a day. The main focus of media is to sell advertising slots.

What are we putting in our heads? Because of my fears, in my first night in the psych ward I had to have someone comfort me to sleep. Bipolar fear is a complex foe. We need to look at it in new ways to give it less power over our lives. What peace thoughts, actions, and feelings can you grow in your life?

Living with bipolar made me fearless in overcoming obstacles. Many times people have told me that I was brave to do something. I find it strange that they would even think this way. It doesn't seem like a big deal after learning to negotiate the large obstacles of bipolar.

How do we turn fear into a positive side of bipolar? Risk taking comes to mind—we need to rationalize through and minimize fears to overcome their power. Living in the world presents us with fear opportunities to get stuck and replay our past experiences; to blow the present situation out of proportion. We can overcome and see these fear situations for what they are, a construction of our past experiences and memories.

Courage starts with and plays out in our thoughts. You will counter the negative and change your thought patterns. I have had times of fear when I would read a positive scripture over and over: sometimes it worked and sometimes it didn't. We need to get out of our instant gratification viewpoint. The feelings we are stuck in today are last months actions and last years thoughts. It is not instant gratification. How long will it take us to change our illness thinking into gifted feeling? We can learn to feel differently on the spot, it takes practice, but we can and do decide how we feel.

One thing about bipolar, it will allow us opportunities to practice over and over till we get it the way we want it to be. The sooner we start, the sooner we can break out of the negative and fears to experience our true life. Bipolar can be a testing ground for us to work through our hell and to enjoy the bliss of our heaven.

May you grow the courage to surmount your challenges and increase your peace. Meditate on your chosen life now. Leave your stuck patterns of negative behind and blossom in your new ways of present.

Points of thought and action:
#1   Do I have patterns of fear?
#2   How do I prevent fear?
#3   How do I prevent my extremes where fear has the most fury?
#4   Do I need to make an imaginary guide angel to assist me if I do end up out there?
#5   Can I learn to rationalize that most things I fear never happen: to change my focus to good?
#6   (My personal plan.)

EASE THE ANXIETY

Does bipolar promote anxious ways? Absolutely. The flavors and ways of anxiety can be numerous. I find that if I am not looking after myself that I can crumble into anxiety over people encounters.

I can be intense and thorough and driven in my thinking, to the point of dwelling on it. It is in these times that I need to break the anxiety patterns. They can drive me to the point of not sleeping.

I have too much information and I need to process it to be solid in my convictions. It can help to write it down and to exercise. I can sometimes allow people encounters to become an anxiety cycle in me. It helps to talk to someone. I talk to my wife about certain scenarios: she is a built in sounding wall. Sometimes the perspective can be missing for me.

The very reason that I can associate and interact and be effective with people and in situations is my sensitivity. To connect with others through empathy is vital to having a life in the real world.

The flip side of the positive interaction with others is the second guessing and focus on always figuring out all the nuances of interaction with the other person. They will usually have moved on or forgotten, and, in reality, they never experience the full details of an encounter as you or I do.

Medication can give us anxiety. When we are tapering off of our tranquilizer we are craving more of the drug. We can be full blown addicts craving the fix in all levels of our existence, but we can work through our addictive tendencies to eliminate our brain and emotional addictions.

We can separate our addictive sensations and cravings by setting up new paths of thinking. Yes, I do want this tranquilizer. Do I need it? The doctor says I do and my symptoms are still a bit out of control. Does the drug have beneficial abilities for me? I decide that it does. I can make myself anxious in all of these stages of thinking.

I decide to take the drug and accept its good medicine. It will soothe and relax me and I will cast out all thinking about it as a bad substance. I need it to work its good and I am taking it not because of my addiction. It is good medicine that will help me out.

Re-entering society after hospitalization was always a challenge for me. Anxiety would be a constant companion. Sometimes the people I interacted with could see it acting through me and at other times I was able to act free of the anxiety influence. It can be serious to the point of not being able to do anything—anxiety can paralyze us.

I experienced panic attacks for a couple of months. I was transitioning into different work and was taking a one month training program. I found it very fearful to have these attacks. Seated in a loose circle of people behind tables, when the panic came I tended to tunnel downward and focus on the floor, then close my eyes. I was not capable of interacting on any level. I would take the medication and try to breathe. A few times I had to run to the bathroom. The flight or fight reaction can be strong and not worth resisting at times. At other times we need to learn to breathe and focus to alleviate the strength of the panic and anxiety.

I believe that we can get stuck in these patterns of anxiety. What we focus on will grow. Do we just input anxiety signals and experience? Is our glass always empty and breakable? What if it breaks and cuts me, or cuts someone else? What if I drop it? What if what I always thought would happen does happen? If what you dwell on and dwell in does not eventually happen, I would be surprised.

How often do we talk and gossip about the positive things in life? How often does the news talk about a positive story? We have to break through human nature to believe that positive things happen and will happen today. Build a case from a legal standpoint: count your blessings. There is always something you can be thankful for; just like there is always something that we can be anxious about.

How many of these things that cause us anxiety actually happen? Sure they do sometimes. But more often we cause ourselves more pain and suffering by dwelling on this anxious state than from the actual bad thing happening. I have had horrible things happen to me and I got over them. Constantly dwelling on the potential of a negative can be worse than its reality. It is amazing what the human spirit can overcome. You will be able to deal with the challenges as best you can at the time and you will learn.

Naming what you face takes away its power over you. Especially talking to someone about what you face internally can reduce its strength to control you.

Get up in the morning and write down ten things that you are thankful for. Carry this card around with you and focus on it. The anxious thoughts will try to get in and they will—this takes practice. It still gets me sometimes. To me anxiety is a symptom of greater needs within me. Should I really be in this situation? Do I need to drink less coffee and eat less sugar? Am I ready for this situation? I need to eat a healthy meal. I need to exercise. I need to meditate. I need to talk to someone about it. I don't need to hang out with this person. I need to get my head out of this rut of thinking. I need to break free from this cycle.

Anxiety before a performance or task is a positive trait—it can show that we care and want to do our best. We desire to be our best and perhaps the anxiety can be faced by accepting the worst that can happen and then preparing and doing your best. Quite often the worst we can think of is very different than our reality. Enjoy the best that can happen and give thanks for the average. Bad things can happen. We deal with them when they occur. Let's not waste our time by living in the bad before it happens.

I have been stressed in the past to go to work. It helps me to think of past triumphs of work. Sure there will be troubles and challenges, but I will make it through. I always do. What is really important ten or twenty years from now? Will I even remember this event?

Experiences with anxiety can help us with creative pursuits. It will help you as an actor. I have no trouble imagining anxious states to write characters and it helps me to write thrillers to have that edgy pocket to go to. Anxiety can be harnessed to be energy to fuel us; the challenge is to eliminate the anxious circles of thought to think in new ways.

When we work through anxiety and come out the other side, it gives us the ability to recognize anxiety in others; we are not the only ones to go through it. We can empathize and go outside of ourselves and help them feel better.

By recognizing anxiety in others it helps us be stronger friends and leaders of people. We can talk about our anxiety and this helps them and it helps us. We call it what it is, we have no pride or fear about mentioning it. It can help bridge to people and put them at ease.

Points of thought and action:

#1   What am I anxious about?

#2   How often has it happened? How much time do I dwell on it?

#3   What is the worst that can happen?

#4   How can I reduce my anxiety?

#5   How does anxiety help me in growing my compassion and ability with others?

#6   (My personal plan.)

IRRITABLE ANGER

Bipolar can bring out intensities that we have never experienced before. Bipolar can take away our sense of self and impair our ability to see how we treat others.

If you took a hundred people from your neighborhood and kept them awake for 24, 48, or 72 hours, like bipolar sometimes does, do you think that many of them would be irritable? Throw in a few items like poor diet and zero exercise and an item of your own choosing. How about not knowing what is going on inside them—mix in some psychotic and suicidal thinking and it seems to me that something would be wrong if they weren't angry or irritable.

I do not write these things to make excuses, but simply to get you thinking about your needs. It can be scary to experience the lack of control in our lives and in each direction we turn there is nothing that we want or seem to need. We can have zero control. In the midst of the tough times it can be nearly impossible to turn things in our favor.

My irritability seems to be a warning sign that I am not protecting and caring for these areas: adequate sleep, proper diet, exercise, adequate time for self, and communicating with my network of support. If I am psychotic it has its own built in veins of rage—the best is to prevent going there with medication and lifestyle. You may find some of the same triggers and you will have unique ones.

You may need a medication change. Certain medications can cause irritability—talk to your doctor about your irritability. Exercise and relaxation techniques can help.

You may be predisposed to anger with your family heritage—your father would lose his mind in anger, and you lose your mind in anger, but you go psychotic too: that would be challenging and dangerous. You need to take this very seriously with anger management classes and studies, and practice the art of mellowing out. We with bipolar all need some basics of anger management. It can be part of the illness and we need to lessen its effects.

What contributes to your anger? Can you avoid these persons or situations? I can't handle certain people at certain times, I have to walk away. Can you eat or exercise or work physically or have sex to have an outlet for this energy? A.A. takes anger and places it in their H.A.L.T. acronym of prevention warning. If you are hungry, angry, lonely, or tired; you have to remedy these four points or you risk drinking again. This can apply to our bipolar traits and you can add a few of your own for prevention maintenance.

Bipolar can provide irritable anger problems. Do not use bipolar as an excuse for your behavior. Yes it can, and does, control us at times. Forgive and learn from your episodes of anger but do not excuse your future actions—your whole life will be an excuse. When I am bitchy I tend to blame others for my problems. They may have nothing to do with them, yet I lash out in my thinking. I try to always catch it in the thinking stage but sometimes I verbalize it. I find that when I look after myself and nurture good thinking, this blame game rarely plays out.

Maybe all you need is that correct dose of the new medication. Talk to your doctor and network—discover your triggers and tendencies. You may be surprised to discover certain things that play a factor. Advertisements on TV really agitate me on occasion. What are your factors of contribution?

Then we need to strive to reduce and eliminate those exposures to triggers. And if we have to deal with them, we need to train our minds to go to happy places and breathe and accept and play games of it to reward us after the exposure is over. You are an individual and need personalized solutions to your life.

Be open minded and try new things. Less caffeine may help you out. Martial arts or dancing could give you an out and self control—you could perform your practice moves and let the angry energy go. Dig a hole. Go for a walk. Perhaps imagining the irritating person being squashed between your fingers in the imaginary world for a few seconds may help you release his or her power over your life. You are not going to harm anyone in reality. Breathe and let the effect go, even if that person is still in front of you. And for some of you the finger squashing would be a horrible thing—akin to murder.

Talk to your people and research to find techniques of coping that work for you. If you have not dealt with the hurt that was caused to you as a child, and you still have to interact with the person that harmed you, it must be horrible. I'm sorry—please get help and avoid them if you can. Life is not fair when it passes out hurt but we can be beautiful by not passing it on, and changing that hurt into good.

I can be intense at times to get a project done. It is a positive thing but it can turn on me—it is a tough balance. While it helps me finish tasks I need to self monitor my needs and have them take priority over the task at hand. I need to pull myself out before any harm is done. Food is my carrot at the end of my task and it is a means for me to slow down and relax.

When we hit these places of rage, it is designed for physical release— it is all we can do to control our striking out. Turn around and strike your feet upon the ground and go for a run, a walk, climb a staircase. Give that rage a healthy physical release, but not to the point of harming yourself.

Let it go mentally. You have great powers of imagination—trust your mind to deal with it. In the moment you may be pissed off at an inanimate object. Imagine shooting the thing up into the sky and it explodes; and you still walk down the rage to a manageable rumble. But why are you blaming an inanimate object for your troubles? We need to accept responsibility and not be players in the blame game.

This anger irritability is not a fun angle of bipolar but we can diminish its power over us. We used to be hunters, gatherers, and soldiers. You could imagine these powers being useful in the past. But they could be dangerous then and now. Perhaps some people who punch walls should have fewer walls in their lives.

It can still serve some use to us if you channel the energy into something constructive. But please when you are channeling your energy let the negative go—don't intensify it. You could repel people. Breathe and throw it to the side to not harm anyone.

Forgive yourself and learn from the experience. Why did you get upset? How can you prevent it from occurring next time? Can you use the energy to do that good thing for yourself? Play your new positive ways of thinking.

Points of thought and action:

#1 Do I get angry or irritable?

#2 Can I pinpoint why?

#3 What would prevent me from getting irritable?

#4 What can I practice to lessen the severity and let it go?

#5 How can I harness this energy into good and healthy pursuits?

#6 (My personal plan.)

SPIRITUALITY

I have witnessed and experienced an aspect of spirituality among mentally ill people. We as a people group tend to accept the existence of a power greater than ourselves. And many of us believe we can have some relationship with that power. And many of us struggle with this to the point of breakdown.

What is it about visiting the crazy outlands that opens our spirituality? There is more out there than the here and now and what we see. We have been stretched to see and hear possibilities beyond the present reality. Perhaps it leaves a residual opening to another existence.

The psychiatric wards I have been in were not good places of spiritual testimony. There was much talk and witnessing and little peace. Some of us were in there because we could not make sense of the spirituality we tried to live.

For me to live optimally in a spiritual world, I would have to be shut away in a monastery or retreat somewhere. Give me nature and a simple life and a devotion to God and I would be better set. I have trouble mixing our world and the ideals of spiritual pursuits.

The biggest percentage of spiritual people, where I was hospitalized, were Christians. And that is the life I tried to live—so we will use it as an example. Many of the effects are interchangeable with other spiritual pursuits. I lived the Christian life with passion. I learned in the bible that I was to do the same things that Jesus did and I looked around and saw frightened people in the church—we had the holy-spirit to work with and we were scared of talking to non-Christians. Did we really have the all powerful spirit dwelling in us?

Everyone is going to hell that does not have Jesus as their savior? I looked around and did not see that this meant anything. Everyone I saw outside was going to hell and we ate potluck meals and played games and built a bigger church and discussed what kind of flooring to install. Is this not serious? Everyone is going to hell and we can watch videos. How can we spend time or effort on the things of this world: cars, houses, possessions? It messed up my head. I could not wrap it around the hypocrisies.

I tried to live hot for Christ and it was great for a while—then it chewed me up. Intimacy with God sent me into psychosis many times. I would be really close to God and then I would go manic. I became afraid of intimacy with God and had to change my priorities—I had to put my health first before God. You would think that God would look after our health, but it didn't work that way for me.

To live in a spiritual way is a challenge. What we hear is an ideal that is sometimes out of touch with reality. How can we be nice about these subjects? You believe every non-saved person is going to hell. Okay I will believe you by the way you live your life. Do you love them instead of judging? Am I judging now?

I think that we with bipolar have to be careful in approaching spirituality. In our manic phases it can be like throwing gas on a fire. I found great encouragement from church people to embrace my heights and then when I flew too high I was dropped into the hospital. Your experience is different of course.

Going through the bipolar experience opened my belief level to a greater being. It can be messy, yet also a great providence for us to work through to our gift. This open belief level can be used for a surge in hope that you will have better days. Fan your flame of hope and watch it grow. It will give you belief to go for it and live better. You believe that you can be healed and move on from the negatives of this illness.

Whatever spirituality you believe in and pursue, you have to evaluate it. Living a spiritual life should aid you in living with more peace, love and joy in communion with other people. Does it affect your bipolar for good or bad or some of both? For me it turned into more of a negative. I had to change my priorities—I could no longer risk my life approaching the highs. Before every high I became high on God. I had to cool down my life with God to prevent my manias. My life depended on it.

Try and explain this to the church people around you. Few understood it. I felt one hundred percent that I had to walk away from God. I eliminated activities and pursuits that encouraged me to feel great about God, especially worshiping and intimacy. The need for this makes me ponder how much of our God experience is self-driven?

Before I became manic the first time, I prayed that God would take me through whatever was needed to develop me into who I needed to be to serve God. Soon after that I had my first psychotic episode. Was it coincidence? I now feel like a new, improved person for the effects of living with manic and depressive phases. I believe that God gave me a gift of adversity. I would be a different person without bipolar; I would most likely be shallow and have totally different values and empathies.

What do you have to do in your spiritual life? Perhaps you struggle with no hope and feel that the suicide statistic is a given—the next time you slip down you will do it. You have finally gotten your things in order including a method. You have tried the career and material possession pursuits. You have tried sex and love and travel. Nothing in this world of commerce gives you hope.

Maybe you need to embrace your spirituality, something powerful outside of yourself to grant you a glimpse of hope and peace. Without hope, depression is your death. It will be the only solution.

In spite of walking away from God, yes, you can say God was always with me; I always had a slight dose of hope. I could always put suicide off till the next day. I did not think well when I was depressed but it was more rational than my heights of mania. Perhaps if I had mixed states when I slipped to my suicidal ideation, I would not be alive today. My mixed states always came on my way past middle from mania. This fact alone could be why I survived. I was not dwelling on suicidal thinking yet. Be diligent in those mixed states.

If you have addiction issues, get your butt to Alcoholics Anonymous or Narcotics Anonymous or something similar. And if you have issues with religions and can't get through their doors, these support groups can be a good entry into spirituality to gain hope and peace. It depends on the group as far as how large a focus it is. Some groups frown on much spiritual talk. Yet the majority of people I met with quality of life in recovery were very spiritual people.

If you have no belief in creation or spirituality, you still believe in something. You still have faith that the chair will hold, the plane will stay up; we all believe. It may be science and explanation. Logic of cause and effect can be a spiritual pursuit—you can control your future with your thoughts and actions. Condition, choose, and harness it to work for you.

Psychiatrists have heard it all concerning spirituality. Our delusions of grandeur in mania can kidnap great religious figures into our psyche. We can be the special chosen one and possess spiritual powers. This is one reason why psychiatrists may discourage your spiritual pursuits— they see the amount of damage they can do. People struggle to live in balance with their spiritual pursuits in the world.

Any hypocrisy, whether it is spiritually based, or a business, or family, can be lived by certain people better than others. Observing hypocrisy and attempting to work through it can cause some people's minds and hearts to splinter.

I think it is a compliment to an individual's spirituality if he or she cannot handle religious hypocrisy. Some people are incapable of deception and when they start to deteriorate, it all falls apart, the crazy hypocrisy jumps out of the cracks. Perhaps this is linked to mentally ill people's tendency to sensitivity. We take the detail and nuances of every emotional experience to heart. We tend to not callous easily. We are fragile. We get chewed up when things collide in sense and personal conflict.

Some man-made spiritual stuff does not make any sense and we are pressured into a square hole—it can be a form of peer pressure. But maybe we are circles and don't fit in the square hole. Others are more capable of ignoring the missing pieces. We keep ramming and those around us keep pushing us. We break off pieces from our complete circle to try to fit. Perhaps those pieces were there for a good reason. We are different people and when I start seeing cookie cutter people all acting the same, it scares me. There are things waiting to get out of them. Is it healthy for everyone to be the same?

Our psychotic experiences open us up to new ways of thinking and experiencing the world. Spirituality must enhance our life and stability to be a vital part of our lives. If we keep hitting our heads against the wall, we have to put our health before spirituality. We have to put our

God in the backseat or trunk if we cannot live with our God in the driver's seat. It can be a matter of life or death.

If you are blessed to live in balance and your faith and spirituality only contribute greatness to your life, I am happy for you. If your bipolar is out of control and your spiritual pursuit contributes to your misbalance, it is your responsibility to do something about it. Talk to your spiritual leaders and make changes to improve your headspace and outlook. You are responsible for your spirituality and how it affects you and yours. If your doctor is capable of the subject, talk to your doctor. More psychiatrists are receiving training in spirituality.

I have heard the acronym G.O.D. means good orderly direction—to live well with bipolar we must have good orderly direction. It is an individual pursuit. You will need to personalize your spiritual pursuit to live in balance.

My spirituality includes good encounters in nature. It includes an openness to others that includes love, and peace and joy. I believe in my community and country. I need to maintain hope in more goodness. My spirituality works best when I take good care of myself.

I need a good spiritual side to live fully in my gift. I believe that I am here for a reason and it is important for me to live in balance and not in illness. Bipolar is an opportunity and being spiritual enhances this seeking of the gift. It makes me fit in better knowing that there is a large sense to be made from this world. It helps me to understand people—to know the controls of greed and lust and other aspects of human nature.

It used to be thought that people who were mad or insane were in special communion with God—perhaps we are; it makes it a tricky place to be sane if you receive special messages from on high. Can you tell others about it? You must talk to your doctor about all nuances of your psychosis—you must get a handle on it. Part of getting to your gift is to give up your highs, you have to not go there, and perhaps you may have to give up your heights with God—they can be intertwined and have a cause and effect action.

I did not want any part of a God that allowed me to go crazy and have to be hospitalized. My God of choice wants me to be healthy, wealthy, and wise. My God wants me to enjoy the gift of bipolar. To be at peace with it and to enjoy all that life has to offer. My God helps me to believe in my bright future. My God gives me ideas to write a book such as this and gives me the tenacity and wisdom to see it through. My God gives great gifts.

Is your spirituality working for you? Does it improve the quality of your life with bipolar? Do you need to make changes?

Points of thought and action:

#1   What do I believe in?

#2   How does it affect my bipolar health?

#3   What beliefs do I need to help me?

#4   What beliefs cause me harm and need to be left, at least temporarily, to get better?

#5   How do I grow hope in my life?

#6   (My personal plan.)

SCATTERED

All these great ideas—and then another one takes you. You just get going on one thing with a certain person and then you are off on another tangent of thought. People can't keep up—it repels them. You are a two-year old's attention span in an adult's body and vocabulary.

Last month I found myself spinning upwards. My mind thought in phrases, not complete sentences, and each phrase jumped onto a different subject with no conceivable connection. My thinking was breaking up and needed a bit of cleaning up with medication.

It snuck up on me and had a negative self-talk angle to it—it came as relief when I realized that I needed to slow my thinking with medication. This occasional surge in different symptoms can be a challenge. We have to be aware at all times of what we need. I had been working a bit too much and not looking after my needs and the result was my skip and pop thinking. I strive to look after myself better this month.

This scattered thinking is at times part of bipolar and can in the end give us great multi-tasking skills. Are you accustomed to looking at negatives from a positive angle? That is what we do by turning an illness into a gift: change our perspective and we change our life.

I found that when I bounced around I tended to be in the hospital and not very aware of time or what I was doing. I had been in a few weeks and had been medicated out of major psychosis and was starting to settle into my body a bit. I was heavily sedated and perhaps that assisted in my lack of time perception.

Later at other medicated manic times when I was on less sedation medication, I think I clued back into the reality of time and this bouncing around that much faster. This is a point to emphasize proper dosages of medication and not too much to the point of delaying the return to a regular state. It is a tricky balance to be worked out with your doctor.

But it is a natural side of bipolar too. Our bodies are trying to tell us something—perhaps they are trying to catch up to all the wildness in our heads. Perhaps it is a bit of a mental hangover. Maybe it is a way to get back into focus. Scattered thinking and conversation is there for some reason: many of us have it. An engine can sputter and run rough when it is warming up from being cold. And our minds have been beyond cold.

There was a point in this post-manic phase when I would start to come to my sense of awareness. Maybe it was important for me to try ways to engage back into this world. I was practicing ideas and eliminating what did and didn't work. Maybe it was very important. Maybe we should embrace it instead of avoiding it. What are your inclinations on being scattered?

Meditation skills and practice can help you focus your thoughts. I find it easier at certain times to discipline my thought patterns. Sometimes I can control them and at other times medication is the only answer.

I think the key is to have healthy pursuits to jump around to that cause no harm, particularly ones with some physical outlets. And when we are well we can use this ability to jump around to converse with many people at once: there are many pursuits where quick changes in thinking are advantageous. When you live in balance your mind is still able to be quick, yet more effective.

Making minute connections between subjects can make me a better writer. You can be a more effective brainstormer to formulate solutions for business and engineering. Your mind is capable of rapid complex thought patterns and even the apparent lack of patterns will assist you in ways of which you may be currently unaware.

Turn scattered inside out and use it for good.

Points of thought and action:
#1 Do I experience times of scattered thought and speech?
#2 What do I think causes it?
#3 What things would prevent it?
#4 What would allow it to have healthy release?

#5   How does it help me?
#6   (My personal plan.)

GIVING UP YOUR HIGHS

After spending months in the depths of depression, I always wanted a change. After the blues I liked my highs. I needed them, I wanted them: it is amazing to live large and not be suicidal and depressed.

Life was sweet and worth living again. I didn't have to act. It was great to string thoughts together and to want to be with people again, to be able to drive under an overpass and not want to run into the concrete wall. What could be wrong about feeling great? I smelled, tasted, heard, felt, and moved better.

And then I soared too high and my wings burned and my head twisted in psychotic fumes. I crumbled and flirted with death. In my last major psychosis I waded into an icy cold river up to my waist and attempted to perform a back flip. I landed on my head on the bottom rock and tore many of the muscles in my neck and shoulders; I floated down the river in great pain.

I had become a danger to myself: I had to give up my highs. It would help limit the depths of my depression. I had to kill the manic darling before it grew too large to control. How does one develop the wherewithal to counter the creature that rises in one's head? But it must be done at all costs.

I studied my cycles and tendencies and learned to guard my sleep. If I slept I could prevent slipping up. I had to limit the stimuli that made me high. When my thinking cranked up and it was going to be an all night session of thinking, I had to hit myself with tranquilizers. If I became psychotic, I had to take anti-psychotics. I would get or take my injections to throw another cover on.

I had to stop going to church and embracing the highs of Christianity. I had to change my spirituality to be a solid anchor, a positive approach.

The interesting thing about giving up my manias was that I missed the adventure and strange loss of control. I started to watch weird movies, including horror, to take little trips—it took the edge off. I have more of a desire to travel to unusual places—even walking a different way home is a good thing, a back alley can be an adventure that helps keep me interested.

Are you like many bipolar people and have to give up your highs? Perhaps you do not go full-blown psychotic but you have to deal with the manic tendencies of excess spending, sexual encounters, and a dangerous spirit. You will have to practice controls on these potential negatives and you may have to give up your highs.

I have developed safe arenas of play for my manic child. It is allowed to play in arenas of creative pursuits: playing guitar, writing, cooking, working on the house and yard, photography, and painting on occasion. I let the child in me play and laugh with friends and family. There are certain toys that he is not allowed to play with. These include: spending to excess, sexual excess that is negative, and dangerous pursuits.

It is not worth it to frolic with the classic mania traits. I am happily married; I do not want to give that up for sexual encounters. I don't want to blow all of our money on stupid things. At times I only have certain access to our funds.

You know whether your manias are dangerous or not. Who wants to lose your mind in psychosis and take months to get back in your head? Is it worth it?

When you work to give up your highs, idiosyncrasies will pop up and surprise you. I never expected to grieve the loss of the psychotic tinge. You will have to be honest regarding your roadblocks with yourself and your support team. It could be that these manic phases are you getting back at your dad who drove you to his idea of success. You hated that he pushed you to be a doctor; you want to be a psychiatric nurse instead. And you became bipolar and you have slipped comfortably into the mould of illness because it keeps you from having to confront your father.

The complexities of your life wrapped up with bipolar may be a tangled puzzle. Keep your eye out and be ready to work through any problems. Use your great attitude and perseverance to knock your walls down. And there may be no particular reasons why you have been holding on to your illness: you just haven't gotten it together yet—it takes time.

I have found that certain friends and family of mine became accustomed to the illness me. Now I am changing more and they don't know me; they want the old dependant Arlen. They are unsure about the independent man who is trying new things. There could be someone on your support team that helped you out greatly through your illness and toward your gift, and now you don't need to talk to him or her like you did for years. This person has lost the role of helping you and now it could be a challenge to know how to relate to each other. I have had this very situation slip up on me—I have just become aware of it.

It is a challenge to keep up to our changing moods and interests and pursuits. I've tried a lot of different things for recreation and money. Some things have stuck and the rest have slid away. And our relationships are affected by these wanderings in our soul: we do transform into different people.

My extrovert in mania was an extreme opposite of my introvert in depression. We are not socially accepted with this savage energy acting out. I have learned and experienced amazing things with my manic side but I've had to bury it, and with time I remember the good things more than the pain and suffering. When I start missing my highs I have to remind myself of the painful horrible events of my manias. I have welded new circuits in my head, warning lights go off at certain points: one night without any sleep—beep, beep, beep: the defense needs to get sleep.

It is a challenge to kill the negative of mania and to be left with positive traits. But I now have the extrovert power to interact with people when I need to. I have great perseverance from living with all aspects of bipolar.

I needed to give up my highs to have a balanced life long enough to grow accustomed to the gift. What do you need to do with your hypo and mania? You may need to eliminate all sugar and caffeine. It might be ten years since you even had a little positive hypo to work with—you have been muted by too much medication. Perhaps you need to talk to your doctor to regain some nice moods of life and pleasure.

For me, normal often includes feeling great and wanting life to last a long time.

You walk a different path than anyone else and you must become aware of who you are and where you need to go, and how. Honing and disciplining your manic side pays dividends in mastering the gift of bipolar. It is our ability to go comic book—yet we have to live without that side of us. But hold on to some of that huge potential of mania. Remember how it felt to be invincible and able to talk to anyone about any subject? With your potential in balance, respect the potential danger.

Don't let the beast rise. Keep it as a humble happy creature and channel it in some productive direction. Use that power to start singing again or walking daily. It is your personal tool to enhance your life. Kill the manic psychotic beast but bottle a bit of its blood in your mind and let a bit out at a time. Remember that it is lethal and dangerous and respect its powers.

It can take you for nasty rides if you give up the reins—it can gallop you to Crazyland and leave you there naked and bleeding. You have to be hard and tame it down to a pony ride—there are certain routes that you need to walk in.

Talk to your doctor and support network—they will observe things in you that you may not be aware of. Use their wisdom and advice to change your life to not include manic highs. You may have to get a different job. You may have to stop exposing yourself to any negatives on how the environment is in trouble at the hands of man. You are an individual with unique triggers and doorways to blow open your manic vistas. And it may take some time to close these doors and dismantle the triggers.

Any progress, even the smallest that you can make in this direction will pay off hugely; especially if your life has been disrupted by mania. Remove a bit of that and you will be amazed at your new life. It may be like your old life in great ways and it may be totally new. You are on a grand adventure called life.

Yet much of life can be mundane, and that is part of the secret to fully opening your gift—we have to embrace the mundane aspect of everyday life. After our heights of adventure, life can pale as not worthy. Try something new. Spice up your everyday: turn the fun music on, get in better shape. Love your significant other and edify him or her to new places.

Celebrate your accomplishments. You have always wanted to go somewhere but you always manic spend and find yourself with the stupidest products. If you stop buying those silly things and get control of that manic tendency, you can save up and be able to go on that trip. We are responsible for the potential disease that wants to take our good life away.

I believe that you have wonderful tendencies within you because I know the themes that bipolar encourages. Mania provides us with opportunity and vast possibilities. It is our challenge to tone it all down into a manageable pursuit of life. You will need to develop unique solutions for your situation. I believe that you can do it—your depressive tendencies can develop great abilities within you to problem solve. And recovered mania keeps you in touch with a great energy. Are not all problems solved with the tenacity and perseverance to find the solution however long it takes? Your energy and wisdom will help you get to where you need to be.

When I think of my life had I not lived with bipolar, I shudder. Now I could not have it any other way. I would fight to keep this bipolar in my life. It has become the best that I am. It has been quite a ride and giving up my highs was paramount in getting to my gift.

We have to be willing to give up our highs in order to be in the right balance to keep our gift open. This will reduce our resulting swings into depression from mania. What do you need to do?

Points of thought and action:
#1   Are my manic highs good or dangerous? Do I need to give them up?
#2   Are there reasons I am holding onto mania?
#3   What are my triggers or doorways to mania?
#4   How do I stop myself from going high?
#5   How does my life change as I stop going high?
#6   (My personal plan.)

GIVING UP YOUR LOWS

Do we ever have a choice about sliding into depression or is it always an internal chemical effect? How do we begin to prevent our slides? How could we ever need to choose to give up these rough places of depression? Even our predictable lives in depression can seem like a safe harbor to shelter in.

I am not saying that everyone has a need to continue to enter depression. There are those of you out there that have depression as only an event in itself—it is not preferred by any part of your psyche. It may be easier for you to recognize what your trigger tendencies are and to eliminate them and your depression. Please perform fearless inventories of your life to remove any possible situational triggers.

There may be no trigger at all—chemical depression treated by pharmaceuticals and away you go to live your life. Rejoice that it is chemical and that there are solutions for you.

Simple regrets and not living fully could be a trigger. How are you influenced by your childhood and family? When I was seventeen, my brother and father died nine days apart. I went to a special place of escape that was of my own creation. To avoid counseling, I presented a role that would appease the people around me. I think that my later dwelling in depression was in a small way a point of avoidance for me.

Yes my depression was chemical and natural and brought on by my illness and imbalance. But there were also situation-induced depression veins for me. And the chemical and situational intertwined. It can be intricate. When I went manic I did things that I regretted. Did I really need to suck that woman's nipple in the psychiatric ward? I would never be attracted to her otherwise. It tasted heavily of soap. In my depression following that hospitalization, I dwelled on it and kept kicking myself.

I had to learn to forgive myself for the things I did when I was high. I had to stop slipping to mania and performing those regrettable acts in the first place. It can be tiresome to always be resisting our natural tendencies with this illness. But we have to get to the gift.

What are your triggers for situational depression? Is it going out with that person, you need to dump and move on? Is it racking up your credit cards once again? You now have five thousand dollars worth of hats. I remember having deep logical needs for buying certain items. Later I did not think the same about the purchase. Depending on your financial situation, a few purchases can send you into a hole. I have suffered in limited money for food because of silly purchases. My manic spending contributed to my anchor of depressive thinking.

Like mania, we need to recognize if there are any emotional reasons depression benefits us. This will be hard to make sense of and will take time. It may be difficult and painful. It is brutal to realize twisted self-sabotaging ways within us. Some of your support group may be intertwined within this. It is essential for your quality of life to deal with all of your past that haunts your present existence.

Are you harboring any issues by having a reason for wanting to be depressed? It can be complex. It may be your mind's way of garnering that attention. When you were growing up, your parents loved you best when you were sick and they helped you out. This is not why you are bipolar but it could be why you sub-consciously need to revisit the chaos, a deep seated need for love. We all need love and we are all affected by our upbringing.

We have to be merciless. The faster we deal with these potential patterns the quicker we can get to the gift. If your dad was an alcoholic and abusive and you are going to marry an alcoholic who abuses you—hello in there, it is time to take this seriously. There are deep automatic patterns that flow and control us. Are you going to break the mould? It takes considerable work that requires a great support team of professionals and non-professionals.

This searching of our lives can take years. Be gentle and kind with yourself. Celebrate your achievements: going to a counselor for the first time can be the hardest thing you have ever done. One thing I assure you: THESE CONTROLLING UNDERLYING PROBLEMS WILL

FOLLOW US. Until we can deal with them and put them to rest, they will control and throw us around in mania and depression. They will stand as a block to your quality of life.

Have you noticed that being depressed has come into vogue the last decade in North America? How many people experience the real thing? Is the real depression chemical or situational? When does your situational shift into chemical depression? When does your chemical slip into situational depression? It is vital to be aware of these two categories.

What situational events make you feel terrible and can you stop doing them? Does drinking alcohol make you depressed? It is a depressive drug. Does too much anti-psychotic tranquilizer send you into a chemical depression? Now that you are depressed, do you sleep with a prostitute and think it will make you feel better, only to find it makes you more depressed?

Depression is a tricky foe. Does the chemical or the situational depression come first with you? Do you even have a mixture of both? For me, I changed over time with my ratios. I could recognize two categories of chemical. There is the introduced category of chemical: alcohol, street drugs and prescription drugs, to which you could add certain other drink and foods.

The other category of chemical for me, at times, is sheer body—my chemical bipolar. I slid naturally up and then I slipped naturally down. Once it is happening, it is performing this slide on its own. It could be adrenaline depletion in part—nearing exhaustion without adequate nutrition and rest. If you don't look after yourself, your body will kick in and try to achieve balance itself. Your body says enough and will capitulate and make you stop. Homeostasis is the natural tendency of the human body to live in balance.

We decide to give up our lows: they do not feed us emotionally. We have discovered and developed ways to prevent and lessen our depressive state. We change our lifestyle to eliminate our situational regrets that cause us to stew downward. We learn to forgive ourselves.

Is there life after depression? Be ready for all sorts of new experiences. It can be tough—you may miss the comfortable blanket of numbness. I have at times found it a challenge to not have that escape. I had to learn new coping mechanisms. I had to embrace the mundane in life and put checks into place that prevented me from slipping into depression. I had to avoid the escape of excess sleep and accept my responsibilities.

I had to move on from depression to get my life on track. In this scary world bed can be a comforting place to be. But my gift is appreciated while awake and lucid and facing the world.

Learn your needs and fill them: work out the problems that control you and keep you in sickness. We have to earn the right to have freedom in bipolar—we could have done some bizarre things and hurt people and we need to gain their trust back. It can take time.

I never knew that bipolar would teach me. I thought I knew myself fairly well before, yet it has developed a deeper awareness. It also developed and stretched me in new ways: I am more complex than before bipolar. I have control-freak tendencies and people-pleasing diplomacy tendencies that mix together. It is strange but that's what I deal with at times. The first step is the awareness of the situation. I have to coach myself to lower my people-pleasing and sensitivities. But when I'm tired these traits can take over, and this usually ends in frustration and anger.

Who can you really please? I find at times, not even me. Yet bipolar has made me a better actor and more aware of who I am. I choose to be genuine unless the person I am with cannot handle all of me. Then I tone myself down. I find this easier on my head than being too complex for them and then having to do a little damage control—I can scare people off who are not flexible.

Bipolar has given me much practice in removing myself from a situation, and when I am better I find I can still be removed from proceedings, I am not as emotional and more capable of logic. And then I strive to experience a healthy range of emotions.

Depression is part of our gift. To feel things to the depth of numb abandonment can help us. It can give us a deep level of focus and concentration. It gives me empathy and understanding toward others. I have better relational abilities with people from my depressive experiences.

Depression can develop a better ability to recognize all potential problems in a situation—if we can use our pessimism to our advantage, we can then turn our attention toward solutions, and leave the depression days behind.

Points of thought and action:

#1   Is my depression chemical, situational, or both?

#2   What are my situational depressive triggers and how can I prevent them?

#3   Can I forgive myself for my actions or lack of actions? How?

#4   Are there any reasons I am holding onto depression?

#5   What advantages has depression developed in me?

#6   (My personal plan.)

SELF-MEDICATING

I believe few, if any people in this world have not self-medicated. If you look at it from one extreme, if you choose one food over another because it makes you feel better, that could be viewed as a form of self-medicating. The sun has not shone for a week and it comes out, you want to and do face the sun and absorb the solar warmth and light—your body craves the sunlight to create Vitamin D. That could be viewed as self-medicating.

Who has not done this? I think there are admirable roots to this trait of self-medicating. Your body is brilliant at maintaining homeostasis, its balance. Your mind is no exception—it wants to be in balance but at times it can be hard to recognize what balance and health could even be.

The mind is a complex intricate web. Have you realized that you have been granted the ultimate puzzle? I hope you like a challenge: bipolar will give you a big problem to chew on. And if all of this is easy for you, give thanks that you are blessed to enter into your gift side—but is it as much of a gift if it isn't a struggle? There is a relationship between these two. Sometimes the harder you work for something the sweeter the taste. Close to where I live is a little mountain, and if you drive up to take in the view, you are impatient and the view is okay. But when you walk up, you are in the moment completely.

We talked about addiction issues earlier: we do have our challenges. In treatment we have to deal with addictive substances: using, reducing, withdrawing, and eliminating them when not required. And bipolar itself can change and then we need different medications.

How long have you had bipolar before it was diagnosed? In what ways did you attempt to help your illness by self-medicating? Did you drink alcohol to come down and take the edge off? Did you eat greasy heavy food? What did you do to change or adapt to a mood? Specifically focus on your mood altering for a while and make note of a few of your favorite standbys. Then perform a wider sweep on your life and make note of the things you do and consume and how they affect you.

I like to watch movies. At certain times in my life it was a negative avoidance thing—I would rather live in someone else's life in a movie than face my own. Now I use it to rest my body, relax, explore, and be entertained. Still at times it is largely an escape but it renews me to reengage in my life.

Self-medicating can be observed as an entirely negative point. Before we were diagnosed we did negative things. We had no deep understanding why we did cocaine or booze. We wade into our addiction issues through rehab and support groups. We accept our need for medications and we fight with their addictive properties. And now we embrace our medicines to look after and care for our chemistries.

We can be addicts and have to use to survive. We have to continually beat our addictive side down to a manageable medicine level rather than a recreational use of drugs. And we have to face and make the most of the medicines we are on—we have to enjoy them and restrict our use of them to the level we need. In all of this your self-medicating tendencies are beneficial.

I learned that my keys to freedom and my gift were in self-treating. Empower me and I will show you responsibility. I will control this illness if it takes me years to do it. Help me help myself. I don't want to be dependent on a doctor I see once every month or three for my fluctuating moods. I can and have tracked and know my tendency moods. I have changed my lifestyle to limit my ups and downs. I have let go of my highs and lows.

You have to self-medicate to live well with bipolar. You have to know what you need at any time to move your mood away from the mania or depression you are leaning toward and change momentum toward balance and stability. Having bipolar is not an excuse to run free. Lack of control is not freedom. It is your choice to move toward balance and freedom. You are responsible for your moods. You have a wild beast that wants to run away with your life: we have to tame this thing.

You have to self-treat with exercise. How often is your optimal exercise? And at what intensity do you need? I get to be an unhappy, stressed person if I do not exercise. I self-treat with exercise—the need for it can build up on me but I know it is a constant requirement of mine.

I used street drugs and alcohol to feel better and avoid facing my problems. I stopped doing that; it was not easy. What negative self-medicating do you need to stop? We need to become addiction experts. We need to remedy all of our addictions, including repetitive hardwired emotional states, in order to break free. If we find ourselves visiting the same negative emotional states over and over again, we could have trained our brain to need to repeat those states. We need to intend and learn new ways of thinking and feeling with our support people.

What treatment measures do you need to embrace? Have you accepted your need for medication? Sometimes when you accept and work with your medication you can taper down their quantity. And if you make all the lifestyle changes to balance your life, you are a changed person. And if you face your past and your family's affect on you, you are sailing toward your gift.

Some people will have trouble with me saying that self-medicating is the key to freedom with bipolar. All I am saying is self-responsibility with a different word. Self-treating can be better. I would hope that medicating is a good word; and who knows the self better than the self? Or should know? Alright, I agree people struggle with knowing and being responsible for themselves. But we can make progress.

In a consuming culture, the corporate powers that be do not want us to know ourselves—they want to push our buttons. They want us to work more of our life force away to buy that certain label. It is our only solution to happiness and contentment. In a consumer driven society, it is a never-content situation. Our economy would go down the tubes if we only bought what we needed. What are your needs and wants? Is shopping a certain form of self-medicating?

To separate the negative from the positive in the topic of self-medicating, we need to analyze them as to their being needs or wants. And then there is the issue of what is really a need. I will leave that up to you and yours, your team can help you. Perhaps you don't need certain friends that keep you down. Be aware of your needs and wants and how you try to fill them.

This topic of self-medicating is about power, too. Self-responsibility is not welcome in the western model of medicine that I have been exposed to. Certain doctors want to maintain their corner of the market power. Some need us to be ill. Perhaps in our ideal world people can care for their own health with help and focus on prevention.

A psychiatrist who empowered me with a good toolkit of medication and the ability to self-inject set me free. I had to learn to be responsible for my chemistry. I had to self-medicate. I had to treat my thoughts, actions, and chemistry.

Can you learn to be responsible for yourself and your chemistry? You should get to the point of knowing how everything affects your mood. I spent several years in a state of questioning what I needed at every moment to move toward balance and stability. It was a pain at times to be focused in that direction but it is still paying me back the effort. Sometimes when my friends were out having fun, I had to go home early and unwind. What do you need right now to improve your health and outlook?

Our society runs not on prevention, but on band-aid solutions and commerce. For me to live in the bipolar gift, I have to responsibly self-treat. I need to have the wisdom to trust doctors to treat me. I have to know my lifestyle triggers to strive for balance. There are times I need to vent to my support friends and times I need to pray and times I need to write therapy poetry. What do you need to do? I need thrill sports to keep me okay with the mundane in life.

We need to be aware of ourselves to have the ability to self-treat. We need to know what we need, not what the commercials tell us to focus on. Inside, you know ways you need to be treated and pampered. Maybe a spa treatment of some sort is your cornerstone to pop out from a depression spiral. A massage once in a while sets you straight. You live in poverty and I am talking about spa money. It does not take money to pamper—be creative and open to your needs.

The universe is a powerful place. I love to be in the midst of nature—to watch a crazy little bird family take off across the water. Nature retreats are part of my pampering. In my poverty days I was less aware of it but I still went into nature with the means I had—I walked. How do you love yourself? How do you treat yourself with rewards and celebrations? It is your life to party. Abundance is within.

Self-medicating before diagnosis is usually floundering in negativity—but it has positive empowerment undertones that you can develop to move away from illness. Feel the power to move toward good mental and physical health.

Talk to your doctor about your medications and any dosages that you can change to meet your changing needs. Most likely there will be certain medications that need to stay at the same dose and others that could be adapted to suit your needs. This will take time to develop— don't expect too much too soon. Communicate and act responsibly and you will be treated responsibly. We don't see our doctor every day unless we are in crisis, but our chemistry is affected daily and our responsible tools to balance ourselves need to be assessed daily.

You can get to know yourself better and be aware of your needs. You can make constant choices to stabilize your moods, make lists to counter an attack. When I am slipping high I: breathe, exercise carefully to not overdo it, relax, believe that I can slow down, take my medication to guard my sleep, talk to my doctor, reduce my stimulants, and listen to relaxing music… Your list will be different.

When I am slipping low I: breathe, exercise carefully to not overdo it, relax, believe that I can raise my mood, forgive myself for any negative actions, play different tapes in my head, don't drink alcohol, take a nice bath and stare at a candle, take my medication, talk to my doctor… You can keep your prompt lists in your pocket at all times.

You can write yourself 'get balanced' cards in advance. Encourage yourself—few others will be aware of how tough our road is. We have to do the majority of this on our own. Our lifestyle awareness and performing can set us free from hospitalizations and illness.

Remember to continue your number system charting: cross-reference these two. When you hit a certain number up or down, it needs to be automatic that you take out your balance card to do certain things, such as take medication. It may prevent you from the next step. You need to work out with your doctor at which points you will automatically contact him or her.

You will impress your doctor with these topics. This is vital information, especially when you are starting out. To me suicidal dwelling, not sleeping, delusions of grandeur, uncontrolled spending or sexual encounters, could and should all be contact-my-doctor time.

Ask your doctor what you should do if things get ugly—as in I want to kill myself now and I don't care about someone having to deal with the consequences of my dead body; but I can't get an appointment to see you for four weeks. What is the emergency protocol with your doctor?

Remember that the "Never Cry Wolf" story can play out. You must strive not to mess with the seriousness of these emergency procedures—make good and certain with your support network that your situation is serious and falls past the 'get an appointment' stage and into the check into emergency—or whatever you and your doctor agree to.

It can be tough to nail down how serious your plight is without involving others. I would have the tendency to cut myself off from others and just go psychotic—I danced the cracks of a higher plane. Involve your support network if you can. Try not to suffer. After my back flip in the river, I would not go into the hospital, and did not involve anyone for a couple of days. I reached further breakdown and had no place left but the hospital.

Retraining your mind is a powerful but elusive tool when you are first starting out. It is tough to be aware in your head. I know how messed up my brain can get at certain times. But strive to be able to recognize when you are slipping up or down and to take out your balance card or prompt list to perform your proven lifestyle choices to help you get back toward your healthy middle ground. Feel the power you possess to live your life and make choices.

Unplug from the media a bit to develop some of your awareness. Study your needs in the library. Our corporate profit runs on rampant lack of discipline and thought. Do they want you aware of how you spend your money?

Use everything around you for your benefit. Engage in your head and walk away from numbness. You have to face your past and how it haunts you through this day. You are responsible for your thoughts and actions. You can change your thoughts and play different tapes. Listen to audio books from the library; make recordings of your own to burn through your problem thinking. This reprogramming is self-treating. Thoughts are more vicious and powerful than drugs.

Treat your very thoughts to improve them. You can choose better attitudes and live a better life. Your resulting emotions will astound you and be a medicine to your soul. You will want to continue to live your new way and feel even better about yourself. Feel the gift of life the way you should live it.

Points of thought and action:

#1 Have I self-medicated and how?

#2 What negative self-medicating or treating do I need to stop?

#3 What do I need right now to change my mood and be more balanced?

#4 How can my doctor empower me with medication to a more balanced life?

#5 Make balance prompt cards of actions for when I am slipping high, low, or into mixed states.

#6 (My personal plan.)

SELF-AWARE TO POWER

A major theme of this book is self-responsibility. You will live in harmony with others if you are true to your self and your needs. This is respect and community. You will speak to others that harm you and you may choose to eliminate harmful people from your life. This can be your age of enlightenment to be transformed to health.

I have worked hard to know bipolar illness and how to transform it into a gift. I am forty-three and still have major flashes of sense regarding getting to know my situation—will it ever end? My major foe has not been this illness but my deep self, developed through my upbringing. It is where much of my conflict ambushed me in controlling how I responded to this illness.

It took years for me to figure through my head and reality. I had some deep-seated right-to-live issues connected to wanting my dad to die when I was seventeen—and then he did die. I avoided facing this responsibility issue and it endangered my life. Of course I would have problems with my self-esteem and feeling like I deserved a good life—I deserved problems, and that is what I lived.

I eventually wore my way through. A breakthrough occurred when I was psychotic in Cuba. I conversed with my dad in the mirror—my eyes were his and he set me free to live my life. I write about it in *Fracture: A Memoir*. You could argue that it did not happen. I am sorry if you have a hard time accepting, and it's a need of yours to discount things that help other people out. Who cares what happens if it helps and does not hurt anyone?

I talked to my dead dad in a mirror in Cuba. And it worked for me, I was able to let go of the guilt I felt and move on. It was my last major psychosis. I had a minor one the next year that was just positive weirdness—the delusions came on hard but I did not crack up. It makes me wonder if my psychotic episodes were my mind's way of achieving homeostasis. Perhaps my inability to sort the problem out in a sane mind drove me into insanity to find solution.

Did my dad really appear? To me it was a concrete experience, it had a profound effect on my psychosis—it lessened and I was able to re-engage with my social group. I finished the remainder of the trip and returned home to not enter the hospital. It broke my dependency on running into the hospital for help. There was a paradigm shift to never be hospitalized again in over ten years, nor to have a major psychosis.

I had thought that I was healed and through and over the experience of my dad. I did not know I needed to talk to him—it was a tough ride into insanity but there was a gift waiting there just for me. I opened it. What lurks in the recesses of your mind? What blocks your life to be lived fully? Imagine having a father who only recognizes success as adequate for praise. He dangles the carrot—he lines your life out through being a lawyer and becoming a judge. All the while you are a judge, in a position of power only because of the carrot your dad dangled for his own ego and desires.

He played you like a puppet to feed his glory. Are you healthy? Did you have to let your dreams die along the way? At what point did you push your dreams so far down that you lost touch with them? Do they cause any ill effects to this day? Does it cause you unhappiness and give you a need to binge with booze or trips or shopping?

It is a struggle in our society to go our own way to discover our needs. We are taught to conform and ignore our individuality. To get to know ourselves we need to be brave and walk into our wilderness—against the grain. It can be a lonely pursuit, but we can build as much support as we need. It is up to you to face your demons down and rise to new heights. It takes time and kindness and courage to face your true self. It is brutal to wade through addiction issues and have to use addictive drugs to live with bipolar—but you can do it with help and perseverance. It is a tough road to clean the corners of the self.

We need to develop early recognition of our slide up or down. We need to focus on identifying our thought, action, and feelings to be up, down, psychotic, or mixed states. The first step is to know which direction we are headed—then we can learn and apply our strategies that counter the upward or downward slip. Our support group and professionals can assist us in this essential goal of awareness—it is one of the keys to set us free. What direction are your thoughts taking you?

We can take control and live life the way we dream of. We can change our thinking. We can learn to dream again. Society, through mediocrity and the mundane, tends to keep us numb to self-awareness yet it is a vital skill that we can develop. Bipolar gives us more opportunities to practice. Our life depends on it.

To leave the illness phase of bipolar and to enter the gift is sheer rebellion. To be healthy and alive and happy with the gift of bipolar you are a rebel of the finest sort. You have said no to illness, a deprived existence, and the weak dependence on the medical system: they will only take you so far. You were brave, you are brave to forge ahead and break through into your promised land.

The world around you will be a better place. Chances are you will contribute to your society in great ways. I believe our walks into the lunatic outlands provide us with great approaches to life. We have been where few have trodden and we do not come back empty handed—it just takes time to make something out of it. How can psychosis be good fortune? It is all in the way you look at it. Roll it around and forget about it, it may make sense some day.

To be true to self is the greatest wonder. I believe in the goodness of bipolar and the great things it has developed in you. To be an extrovert on command is brilliant. To be creative with the courage to go out on a limb and receive new writing or paintings or business solutions is gifted. I have read of bipolar people who are wonderful inventors. Solutions are discovered through openness and the trust to be courageous to receive and develop from problems or sheer nothingness. Our thinking tendency of skipping around can be utilized to focus abstractly on various facts of a problem to synthesize a new solution with a novel twist.

Your solution lies within you. You have to take missions into your inner world to remove the illness and gain footing into the gift. It waits for you but will not be handed over easily. This gift is a reward for great struggle and achievement. The emotional and mental challenge hoops in your head are greater then any tests the great universities of the world will give you. You are beyond their doors: this is the ultimate bipolarate thesis.

For you to face bipolar fully and break through from illness into gift-hood, you deserve accolades. Feel them now. Feel the goodness of living in balance and the enjoyment of your dreams and full potential. I am there too. Come and join me in happiness and contentment. What a wonderful world we create for ourselves. You are the creator of your existence and environment.

You can change and grow through facing yourself. It can be scary—remember it is your place and only you can do something about it. You can and possibly did create and accept and protect your living hell; you can break down its walls and grow your garden of possibility—feel the power to change your life to what you want and need to live.

It can take time, be patient and take small steps.

Points of thought and action:

#1   How am I responsible for myself?

#2   What do I avoid dealing with?

#3   Can I face bipolar to a balance?

#4   What is unique about me?

#5   Why is responsibility good?

#6   (My personal plan.)

STIGMA

We can carry the mark with us—people can see us as scarred. They see us act in awkward manners and they will remember that more than any goodness we have displayed. When will we as bipolar people shine our gifts fully for people to appreciate? The world is a better place with bipolar. Perhaps we need to advertise the many accomplishments and contributions that bipolar people have given to us.

The media presents bad aspects of the illness of bipolar more than the gift side. Most people have negative ideas when they hear that someone is manic-depressive or bipolar. We are branded by perhaps the one negative experience that the person had. Meanwhile they are unaware of hundreds of positive experiences with the gift side of bipolar.

I met with an employment counselor a while back and he had a story of a bipolar co-worker who was difficult to deal with. This painted the counselor's view of me. He did not know me, yet he was tainted by one bad experience. I challenged him and asked if he had ever had any bad experiences with other co-workers. He smiled, he had. I asked him if he carries those negative experiences with him to judge those people types. He appeared to see the light.

We are scarred with terminology. Mentally ill is a bad term to focus on. Would anyone say they are physically ill? We are scared and goofy around the whole subject. We don't want to offend people so we use the generic term mentally ill—it sounds like a term of pity to me. It is also a focal point: think on illness and you will always be ill.

Ignorance and fear drive stigma and prejudice to bad places of incoherence and lack of logic. Ask ten people what bipolar or manic-depression is and they will struggle with an answer. I find the tendency is to focus on the depression and resist the other side of the equation. I watched a movie with a manically depressed robot character. He was cute and funny, yet he displayed more pessimistic traits than any depressive; and zero manic traits. People are scared of what they don't know and they make things up.

Unless a physical illness is contagious one is safe. It can even be comforting to label people with the illness name. Perhaps it goes back to our survival days—if someone is lame and physically unable, they are not a threat to you. Yet a mentally ill person is a perceived threat—the media of movies and news reports drive this fear and throw a wedge between us and most others.

Perhaps this is our future: we bipolar people need to educate the population on what we face and what we offer from our gift realm. I feel sorry for so called normal persons that have not experienced the poles. I have lived the ultimate adventure in my head and sorted through to make a great life for myself.

I have surged with extrovert bridges to inaccessible souls. I have walked on mountaintops and soared the heavens in time travel. I have felt like a God and used the power. I have slept in the corner of a depression cave and worshipped the method of suicide—I have escaped into my created dream world and hidden from reality. I have felt the heaviness of the depression blanket.

As the positive in bipolar comes to the forefront, we will have a better world—and it would be easier for future people to leave the illness behind and focus on their gift. Do we tell people that we are bipolar? Sometimes I do and sometimes I don't. Do we gain anything with the telling? I read the person. On occasion it can take a long time for me to decide, but I do not feel truly in sync unless they know this is who I am. I like to sell people on my good traits before I tell them.

On occasion I do not tell people because I observe them and decide that they are backward and unable to handle the truth—sometimes years later they can know but they are not ready for it. This is all right. There is a time for everything. In my negative years more people knew about my bipolar than in my positive years. When we are in our illness stages we often do not have choices of who knows and it can tend to be negative. Our life is a mess and people label us and we promote the unstable negative. This is all right, it has happened and is reality as we know it—water under the bridge.

Some people will be driven away by your actions and behavior. It could be loved ones. This is extremely difficult. What can you do? Some things will never be the same. You are a changed person. How you face the stigma of your relationships can cause you to get stuck in a rut of illness.

You can have stigma against yourself—and rightly so, you should. I was upset to have this illness. I was angry and screamed and yelled. I grieved the loss of my life as I knew it, and so should you—I give you permission and encourage you to grieve. Part of getting through this is to bury our past self before bipolar; we have to accept that we are not the same. This will seem like a horrible thing at first—all about our past so called normal existence is great and nothing about our illness is good. Grieve it however you need to. Stoic stone response will keep you frozen and cracked. Give yourself permission to feel your experiences.

We will be the same yet enhanced. Depending on the ratio of illness to gift, it could be viewed as enhancement or impairment. Forgive your stigma—forgive those who hold it against you and are prejudiced; you need to forgive your self for judging your own bipolar illness. If you are diagnosed truly as bipolar, and you believe it yourself, you have to wrap your head around that.

This topic of stigma may throw major problems in your direction—your husband may leave you and take the kids in your time of psychosis. How do you get over and through this? I feel for you, do you feel for yourself? You have a tough road ahead. The amount of time you spend with your kids may depend directly on your ability to leave your illness phase and enter your gift of bipolar. Time is our friend and we can stabilize with age—our approach changes the speed that we can move on from the negative illness effects.

Acceptance is a major step. Once again we move toward self-responsibility and self-treating even on the subject of stigma. You can feel and live in the role of stigmatized victim for as long as you want—you can be the martyr. Yet you made it this far in the book—I think you are past this stage. We all have to work through our persecuted victim stigma phase. What do you need to do or accept to move on from this place?

You will have to leave certain people behind—are they truly your friends? What is love but acceptance of who you truly are? It is important to be kind to yourself. In the early stages there is little or nothing positive to be found in this illness—it stinks. I have left certain people in the past. It was hard. For me this has been part of my experience of stigma. Pick and choose your team to play life. It's your choice. People choose us through stigma—they cast the spell on us and sometimes it is not worth the effort to work through the negative focus of this judgment. And at other times it is very much worth involving your stigma person, with you leaving the illness and sharing the gift with them. It can be a challenging and fruitful journey to health.

Perception is huge in our world. What is the perception you project into the world concerning bipolar? It is partially our fault why the stigma working against us even exists. If you are not coming to grips with responsibility for your internal and external world, that is what you will sell to your circle of influence. They can reinforce your sick approaches and acceptances. Voila, you have a nice little circle of repetition of your illness, your circle of people treat you as ill and you take the role on with relish.

Be aware that you have control of stigma against your bipolar. You have more power than you realize. Every word you speak and the attitude you cultivate changes your existence. Be aware and responsible for stigma in your life. Our greatest ally in stigma would be to leave the victim role, accept the illness, learn to reduce it and take on your life. It will be the hardest thing you have ever done, but the dividends will surprise you. My life is paying off, the toil that I bled a decade ago is returning to me as extra momentum. The wind blows goodness to me now. Twenty years of struggle is paying off. There are times when the cruise control carries me. And sometimes it is horrible, but now that passes quickly.

Early on in my illness, I wanted a certain job; it was something I thought that I could do in my strong phase of year—a summer seasonal position. I approached the man and felt that I should not mention that I was manic-depressive. I worked the position for two summers. I performed my duties with excellence. I eventually told the man of my condition—it may have been in the second year.

At the end of my employment I asked the man for a letter of recommendation. It was a good letter but jumping from the page was the commentary of my not telling him of my condition. It was an unusable recommendation letter. It confirmed the fact that I would have not gotten the position if I had been honest. My gut feeling had been correct.

It bothered me that I thought I had done a good job and he expressed it in the letter but he spoke of my deception. It is a tricky subject to address. I have had many jobs since and I tend to be a coveted employee. I work hard with competence for the task. Usually I have not let employers know of my condition. I have found that it can complicate the matter. How many people have I showed good work to and not used the opportunity to show them the gift of bipolar? Too many.

I had a few jobs where I was honest—it was in my early days and the illness jumped up and showed its head. In each case my employer showed compassion and wanted me to continue as an employee in the future. In the one job that I did go back to for a term, I found it liberating to have them in my loop of awareness—they knew my secret and it gave me support and encouragement.

But I moved on to different jobs. I have a voracious appetite for experiences and learning—I have worked at many jobs and am thankful for this. Bipolar has given me traits and skill sets that are extremely functional and adaptable to workplaces. Even the living through psychiatric ward experiences has prepared me for certain work environments.

I tended to go through a phase with many jobs where I was less interested: "This is all there is to this place?" I find writing to be my ultimate challenge, and it is one of the reasons I write. Writing provides plenty to chew on. It scares me to face the challenge of pulling a book or screenplay off. I love the thrill of writing fiction—my experiences with depression and psychosis enable me to trust the path of story and characters; and events are more organic because of my experiences. Those fractures and shafts of insanity opened up fertile ground for creation.

I have journeyed through stigma. My writings tend to have bipolar content. I am finally at the point where I am jumping out of the closet. It is my gift to write and be me. Here I am, take it or leave it. My writing helps the cause of understanding bipolar. I would not have written this book if I was not bipolar and this chapter is better for me having experienced stigma.

A few years back I was van pooling to work and one guy mentioned that his mom happened upon an accident on the freeway the evening before. His mom worked as an ambulance worker but was on her day off and was one of the first people on the scene. There was a young woman crumpled in the ditch screaming, "The glass, the glass." Her head was swelling and the young woman's mom helplessly kneeled. The young bipolar woman had jumped from the vehicle driving seventy miles per hour. She was screaming, "The grass, the grass." It was poking her wounds.

This story makes me cry every time. What was she going through to jump out? I would guess psychosis but maybe mixed states? Was she newly diagnosed? Did she have the proper help? Six people in the van heard this story of bipolar and they did not know that I was bipolar. Did I help her soul out by keeping quiet in that van? She did die. May this book help prevent the same from occurring. Her poor mom, may she find healing.

The simple fact of us being bipolar can bring us harm—sometimes it is best to stay quiet about it. May you have the wisdom to know when you can talk about being bipolar. There seems to be more talk by people when they are experiencing the negative struggles of bipolar.

There have been times of employment where I have been curious about another person—someone who seems bipolar but I can't ask them. I propose that we have a secret greeting. I draw or make a circle of some kind. The other person, if he or she is bipolar, will draw or make a stick figure of a bird in flight along the circles equator. We then know that we are safe and can talk about it. In certain circles this would keep our employment and business positions safe. This is a way of building strategic alliances.

We can show our community the gift side. I look forward to a bipolar pride day. It is the first day of spring. The basic celebration is for you to inform someone, who doesn't know, that you are bipolar. Mention some advantages of being bipolar—how it has helped you out. You still need to be careful who you tell. It is a great day. What a wonderful way to combat illness stigma. Spread the word about bipolar pride day being the first day of spring.

Take creative initiative in your community in expressing bipolar pride day. We will inundate the media with the great accomplishments of bipolar people. We can advertise the advantages of bipolar. Let's inspire a new way of looking at bipolar. Organize a walk with it culminating in an open mike discussion about bipolar. Let's grow the positive community awareness of bipolar enhancement.

In a couple of decades we could turn this thing around and have a reverse stigma—we could get it to a place where people wanted bipolar and the gift. They would recognize that we live with advantages. We have a famous children's author that talked about his manic psychosis being an inspiration to his ideas for stories. Bless him for speaking out.

What a great world we can create. Let's remove the illness and live the gift. It is our place to remove the word stigma from writing and conversation concerning mental health issues. We will help the new people coming into the fold to have fewer complications in their lives. You can say you are bipolar in any job interview and the people with the power will want to make concessions to have you on board. They will grant us more flexibility to be able to use our gifts for their benefit. What a glorious future we have.

Points of thought and action:
#1   How have I experienced stigma?
#2   What is stigma?
#3   Why am I a better person with bipolar?
#4   Can I accept that I am bipolar and forgive my own stigma?
#5   How does bipolar allow me to live life better?
#6   (My personal plan.)

POVERTY AND WEALTH

The illness phase of bipolar can provide little focus to bring money in. The traits of manic spending and excesses of partying and adventure can drain our funds. Psychosis and depression can leave us in states that do not attract much money. If we stay in this illness phase of bipolar and have no one supporting us and no investments or disability insurance, we may dwell in poverty. This lack of funds can affect our every move.

We may lose our jobs or school focus. We could lose our business. We could blow all our savings and rack up our credit cards. Chances are if you are bipolar you will have had an interesting financial life. Predictable and mundane are not on your chart.

The illness took from me the ability to make money. And then I was able to handle only low stress jobs that paid terribly. I was poor. When I was manic I had a tendency to start smoking, which further taxed my money situation. A pack a day can take away choices of food and the need category, even if you roll your own. What was I to do?

I learned to live on less—I cut corners in every way and focused on my lack and that is where I stayed. I had more time than money or health. I came up with a trinity theory that one needs to be aware of and keep in balance: money, health, and time.

We all know people who make a lot of money and have no time to enjoy it, and wreck their health. They make quick purchases and do not have the time to enjoy them. I lived in an oil patch region for years and was able to witness this among many people. The money flowed but the time was restricted and the health and significant other relationships slid to a lower priority.

I had plenty of time in my illness stage to sort through things and face my situation. I had to live and hold my head up. I found I could only go so far in healing and I had to return to making money. I struggled with my lack of money in watching the world go by.

I had to choose my attitude in spite of my amount of money. This is a tough challenge. People who have a lot of money face the same choice and they may have a disadvantage—they are able to hide in the pursuit, and purchase of the next item or trip. For some it is always hollow chasing, never content. There are very happy people from all walks of life. I believe it is a decision—we have to change our mindset to be content with what we have. Then when we get more, we will still be content.

It is a daunting task when we are exposed to a consumer driven society—from the time we wake to the time we fall asleep, we can be inundated with purchase messages. Look at all these happy faces with their new products and services. The news may instill fear and negativity but the commercial breaks offer us salvation by buying our happiness items one at a time.

A huge aspect of dealing with poverty, for me, was avoiding the shop for happiness ploy. It is my way of being happy. Don't get me wrong, I love to buy things—a little too much at times. It creeps me out how greedy I am. I have periods of wanting everything. How much is enough? I see extremely unhappy rich people—stuff alone can leave your soul empty. And I see extremely unhappy poor people, especially in a place where there are a lot of riches. The envy can come out and play and rot your soul. I really have to work at keeping my greed and desire for consumption in check.

As I struggled and gained ground in leaving the illness regions of my situation, I had more and more periods where I could focus on making money. I forced myself to try new jobs, ones that I hated, just to better my situation. The extra money was useful to climb out of the illness phase. It was a real trade off—at times my health was placed into jeopardy from these more stressful jobs because they took more of a toll. But they offered more to my self worth and granted me more time and freedom to practice my life away from illness.

Money afforded me protections from the illness. I could eat out on occasion and this greatly improved my health—when I was mentally unable to purchase and prepare food, I could still eat.

I did not want to go on disability assistance from our government. Where I was living, it was all or nothing in so far as you were on it and you stayed on it. And the amount leaned toward the nothing, the poverty side. I chose to not go there and instead suffered through higher paying jobs for short periods of time and then used medical employment insurance. It allowed me better health and freedom, and when I had my times of illness I had some money to live a better quality of life.

But I had a cyclical illness that afforded me windows of five-month periods where I could work and there were good paying oil patch jobs that I could get. You have your own difficulties to face, and I believe your own solutions. You have plenty of time and little money but you are a good artist or musician—embrace new ways to make money from your creations. "Necessity is the mother of invention."

You can choose to be happy in spite of your finances.

I've been to the food-banks and dwelled in the rotting canker of poverty. I prefer having money. Can we imagine people from other less fortunate parts of the world being put into our shoes? If certain persons were slid into our situations of subsidized housing and monthly checks of pittance they would be in heaven—they would feel rich. But some of us have slid from heights to our illness and poverty, and it can be a tough fall.

In our consumer-driven society there is a value placed on your life—the more money you have or are perceived to have, the more you are valued and deemed beneficial. Some people will pay you no attention because you will not buy something from them. I like to avoid such places. It is a terrible practice to place your value against how much you can purchase.

I am now eternally grateful, as I pull myself up from poverty, for those years of poverty helped me develop true contentment and values and priorities that don't place things high on the list. I love great things but that is not the be all, end all. You do not impress me with your fancy cars and clothes and purchases. If you are a warm happy person who will interact with me, that is something I value and can take home with me.

I don't think about somebody and their possessions at night when I go to sleep and smile, but I do smile when I think of interacting and sharing something with someone: a laugh, a meal, or a conversation. To me these are riches. I feel sorry for people who are superficial and only focus on possessions. Some people of limited funds are huge consumers—I have seen thrift store gluttony. Everything is cheap and that is the reason to buy lots every week. I have seen people's places crammed full of stuff. It can be a continual chasing after contentment and happiness and it can be a false comfort to be surrounded by material goods. It can keep you from your true intended life.

Our society is focused on material goods. This is one reason why it is hard to enter the gift side of bipolar. Illness thrives in tangents of chasing after happiness in impossible ways. We have to place value on knowing our true needs, and filling these needs. Your health must take priority over money. Eventually more possessions can be the icing on your cake.

People work themselves to death to have more things. Parents allow someone else to raise their children so they can go off to work and pay for babysitting and lose fifty hours of their life force every week just to buy a fancier car. These decisions or acceptance of living can affect our mental health. Have you ever figured out how many hours you have to work to purchase that product that a celebrity makes money pushing? (Remember to calculate your net pay per hour and any transportation costs etc. to work those extra hours.) (reference #5)

Is the other product just as adequate for your purposes at half the cost? You can spend those extra hours with your loved ones fulfilling some of your needs. Please be aware of your money and life force time and where it goes.

Money issues can lurk deep within our living with and holding onto aspects of our bipolar. You could be stuck in your illness of bipolar rebelling against the old money family that you came from. It did not give you the illness—but it could be a way of you holding on to it. Do you want to live in this way?

I have seen wealthy bipolar people who had an easy upbringing where they got away with anything and everything was handed to them: they get the illness and they have a hard time moving toward the gift side because they have little self discipline or drive. Are you hungry to leave your illness side of bipolar?

I guarantee there will be some money issues for you to deal with. Do you know your money spending or hoarding patterns? Do you binge and then have nothing? Are you able to control it? Have you built strategies to counter your manic spending?

Do you pay yourself first? Even ten cents to a savings account—open that door. Maybe you want a down payment on a condo. There may be some ways for you to save some money. Change phone plans. Don't get a cell phone, just get a landline. Or don't get a landline, just get a cell phone. Buy your answering machine instead of renting it. If you have discipline with a credit card, you could get a card that pays you points and make all your purchases through the card and then, this is the key point, pay the card off every month, don't keep a balance. Pay it once a month from your bank account and you will save service charges by not making many transactions. We can make fewer transactions to limit the service charges. I hate paying bank service charges and love anytime that I keep more of my money.

Can you roll your own cigarettes instead of buying tailor-made ones? Can you reduce and quit? Can you buy food in bulk at a cheaper store? You have a unique life with unique solutions. The library has stretched my budget over the years. What stretches yours?

It is important to enjoy your money too. Do you give yourself some play money? Treat yourself.

Do you think we will ever teach the masses to be wealthy? Suppose that you are on a lifetime of disability assistance and you rent your place of dwelling. It makes more sense that your assistance pick up the down payment for your condo and in twenty or thirty years the main portion of your dwelling would be paid for. That would free up more money for them and you. Yet people make good money off of rental properties—the system goes back a long way.

My wife and I attended a Millionaire Mind Seminar where we became aware of the financial patterns that came from our upbringing. We now know when we are acting on automatic negative conditioning. The course set us free to embrace being financially free. *Secrets of the Millionaire Mind* (reference #9) is a book worth reading—it will take you down the same road toward financial freedom.

Many of the people who appear to be the richest in our society are in debt—it can be meaningless as far as net worth to consider a car or house or possessions. Debt is larger than ever before and it comes down from our governments—we have mortgaged our grandchildren's future. Have you ever seen how much the national debt interest payments are?

The Millionaire Next Door book (reference # 6) studied the average millionaire out there and found the model to be one of frugality. These millionaires saved money by not spending much and investing it in a wide range of pursuits. This first generation tended to not enjoy their money much—they simply amassed it and the next generation spent more of it and had their own dependency issues to deal with. The millionaires surprised me in their vehicle choices: a Crown Victoria and F150 pick up were the first choices and were kept around for a while. They focused their funds on things that did not depreciate. Cars turn to rust. These millionaires struggled and bought their primary place of residence and moved up from there.

In this day and age where there are more people coming across large sums of money quickly, these patterns are changing. Some new ways are easy come, easy go. Many wealthy celebrities in sports and entertainment spend for status and some of them fall by the wayside when their money-earning capabilities dry up and they have not educated themselves on developing passive income streams to match their lifestyle.

We are different and have unique situations. For some of us, through our parents' influence, money is evil. The bible says that the LOVE of money is evil. Having a lot of money can be a wonderful power in your life to have freedom to help people out. I believe most things can be used for good or evil. A knife can be used to cook a nice meal or be a murder weapon.

What are your hang-ups with money? I am getting fewer hang-ups and moving toward wealth. We have a rusted car worth five hundred dollars; it gets us to where we need to be. As I polish this book, we have a new used car now, worth maybe 3500 dollars, and it is paid for. Our car has slowed its depreciation. Our house on the other hand is appreciating in value, and it costs the same as renting it. The last new car I was exposed to looked great—it was to be leased for two years, and then the plan was to purchase it. Much energy will be spent on those payments. We have the power to decide what we want to focus our time on purchasing.

I believe in the law of attraction. What you focus your being and emotion on will grow, whether it is good or bad (reference #3). If you focus on the illness of bipolar, that is what you will receive. If you focus on your lack of material goods and your unhappiness because of it—that is what you will continue to receive. If you focus your emotions and attitude on contentment, and happiness, and wealth, these arenas of your life will grow.

I make choices of how to spend my money. Years ago, quitting smoking freed up my funds. Frugality is a wonderful virtue that is to be commended. We all have our splurge areas of spending that others would look down upon. Some people never allow themselves a beverage with a meal out. Some people buy five-dollar coffees. Others collect figurines. We make a choice with every cent we spend. Feel the power to choose. It is a trade with our life, since we exchange hours of our life for cash. How do we spend our life? (reference #5)

I believe one ticket through poverty is frugality and it can be a key to developing contentment as well. If you develop the attitude of joy and happiness with less money, you will carry that great attitude with you as you gain more wealth.

Perhaps instead of eating fast food you could buy some basic vegetables and prepare them to eat raw. You could eliminate your heartburn and have better intestinal health. Drink water instead of sugary drinks—you could stabilize your blood sugar and mood, and reduce your calorie intake.

We live in a world of cause and effect. If you spend your last money on a drinking binge, you not only mess up your brain chemistry to the point of illness, but you have no money for your phone bill. You like to talk to your kid and you feel horrible and slide into depression. What we spend our money on causes effect on our entire existence, including our mood. What we value and focus on will grow.

The Wealthy Barber (reference #7) is a great book on gaining wealth. Its premise is that a barber can become rich and retire earlier than someone who makes many times more money. Spend less and don't waste your money on things that depreciate, invest your money and watch it grow to pay you. Educate yourself on investments that appreciate. Enjoy your money too.

A balanced life living with bipolar means having control of your finances. It is a tough road. Our illness side can spend all our funds on silly purchases. You can start again and enhance your plan into a new focus. You can hand over your financial control to a trusted friend and receive your play or allowance money each week. You can prevent manic spending sprees by cutting off your source—it might only be required for a few years. It is up to you. We are not victims. We have power over our lives.

As we enter the gift side of this illness we can find that we offer the world a unique service. We have been places and developed ways of creation and awareness. If we are true to the gift leanings, it will develop new skills in us. We will change as people and be able to offer valuable creations, services and products to the world. For this we will be compensated more. Ideas can be turned into money.

We can provide solutions that few others can. I have been better paid than my contemporaries because of the very busyness, attention to detail and thoroughness that the gift provides. My challenge is to maintain a balance of health.

I tend to work at an intense job for condensed periods of time and make great money. Work is my main focus at these times. I tend to put a lot into my work and it is good for me to not have many distractions. I work, sleep, and eat. I tend to work more hours for more money and then have time off. It works for me—what works for you? You can get to the place where you make more money in a way that is suited to your needs. We are seeing shortages of workers and if you stand above the rest with your own skills and unique offerings you can receive more freedoms and rewards.

If we wallow in our illness we may always live in poverty—they can go hand in hand. Poverty is not a bad place. You could argue that excessive wealth, depending on what is done with it, is worse than poverty. People in poverty are more limited in the ways that they can help others—time is the main commodity. Access to more money gives freedoms of time and grants more choice. I believe you can be healthier with a little more money, you can eat healthier and have more fun with varied pursuits.

But remember we are all capable of great things. Think of the impossible and do it. Others will try to keep you down and out and predictable. You can do whatever you want.

Bipolar opened my eyes to possibility. I can be wealthy if I want to be and provide something of value to the world. My imagination has been enhanced by bipolar and that is what I am marketing. I love to create worlds of fiction and I intend to be greatly compensated. I want to continue to be happy, regardless of how much money I have. I have enough for my present needs. I will be given more and would like to do some good things with it. Because I have gotten used to living frugally, I don't really need excessive amounts, I will have funds to play with to help people out.

Mania represents unrealized riches—we are open to extreme possibilities. We need to continue to be tapped into that potential as we leave our illness stages and enter our deserved and designed gifthood. Imagine how great it is in your ideal world. Are you open to the universe and what it wants to give you? You will gain independence and will be able to help people. The beauty of bipolar is it teaches the importance of interdependence.

I believe the bipolar experience can be looked at as a test—it is an offering and we can enhance it to achieve our dreams, and blow open any limitations. It is ours to reap what we sow. Leave the illness side and choose to be content and happy with whatever you have and be open to possibilities. That is the key to change your values and priorities to be fully in your life each moment.

There are many ways to make money in this world with ideas and words and creations of thought. My favorite book on the subject of making money from nothing is Napoleon Hill's, *Think and Grow Rich*. Some of it is a little dated but it all runs deep in our bipolar world of enhanced imagination and created ideas paying off. We can make as much money as we decide to. What will we accept as enough? What are we willing to give and create? What we focus on will grow. I pick pennies up off the street. In the last two months I found two American twenties and two Canadian five-dollar bills.

I have read statistics on working and business bipolar people and we tend to make more money than average people. But who cares how much money anybody has? Who cares what kind of car you drive or the clothes on your back? Who cares about your toys? Are you happy? Do you love life? Are you a fun person to be around? Do you have good friends? I will choose fun and friends over money any time.

I continue to keep a healthy balance between time, money and health. It creates the possibility for my greatest happiness. I hope that you are able to continue to change your attitudes to focus on the good and what you need for balance and health and happiness. Money can help us leave our illness side and enter the gift. It can buy us freedoms and give us choices to keep our bodies healthier and our minds clearer.

Grow the feeling of prosperity and contentment—you will attract great opportunities and wealth tangents. It all starts with our thoughts. The only limits are what we accept. We have a large challenge and a great opportunity with bipolar. Seek wisdom before riches. Enjoy.

Points of thought and action:
#1 How has bipolar affected my finances?
#2 Do I value health over possessions?
#3 What safeguards do I need to put in place to protect my finances? (Manic spending.)
#4 How can I choose to be happy and content?
#5 Can I educate myself on the subject of financial freedom: to develop passive income streams to pay for my desired lifestyle?
#6 (My personal plan.)

DELUSIONS OF GRANDEUR

It sounds twisted, exotic, and perhaps even lovely. But it is a frightening place for our loved ones and acquaintances. You are God, you are the chosen one, you have a special mission, and you are going to save the world.

I have felt the special powers many times and I have blundered in communication with others about their own special missions. The sad part about the grandeur is that others just don't see it. They say we are messed in the head, we are ill and that is that.

We need to accept and work through these delusions of grandeur. They can be tough to understand. Talk to your people and ask for their forgiveness and understanding. Forgive yourself for the weirdness. You are not the only one. There is goodness in the midst of this. You want to be more than you are now. This is good. You can move on and leave these delusions to drip dry to dust. You can transform yourself to health and stability.

Anti-psychotics are great for cleaning up these symptoms. Work with your doctor to eradicate the negative levels of these delusions of grandeur. But please leave a little positive opening of possibility. Perhaps we experience these large places for a reason unknown to us thus far. I believe these delusions are helping me develop my writing craft to finish my first books and screenplays. If I had not experienced these delusions of grandeur, would I have had the confidence to attack this book project? Or to approach movie producers and get my scripts read? I believe I have great things to offer the world.

Whatever can be good about psychotic delusions of grandeur? They are all the same and yet different. Always we are more powerful and bigger than we actually are. Wow, this is cool—who do you admire in the world? Is it an entertainment or sports or business creative figure? When they were younger most esteemed people in the world have believed more about themselves. They were nobodies looking up at their favorite heroes. They believed that their lives were capable of greater achievements and places. They went for it and worked hard and became who and where they are now. They needed to dream to take risks.

They believed they were special and capable of unique achievements. They grew tired yet they tried and it grew and they made it and they should feel great about their place in life. Luck is involved but luck loves a person who believes and does not quit. Luck exists where a person makes the best of a situation, where he or she believes all things are possible.

How does this link to delusions of grandeur? If you believe you are God, it gives you practice for possibility in your life. When you settle into reality as you know it, you will have an easier time believing in your dreams enough to make them come true. When you lose sight, you can refocus with a bit of that delusional energy and then change it to reality. Be careful, it is a bit weird—but there is value in it. It's worked for me to get through the last couple of years of writing.

I tried to kill myself once because I was responsible for the destruction of the world. You have to find good in everything to move on. Your negativity will hold you in negative. I need to flip things inside out to see the goodness in them. I must be a responsible person to feel so deeply that I had to commit suicide for what I did.

I hammered booze and street drugs into my system to avoid dealing with my past. But now I can look at it all and laugh—there is good and silliness in it. I have to make light of it, but at the time it was an all-inclusive hell. Hey, it gives me some great topics to write about.

I am different—and in certain ways better—than other people. So what? Everyone has unique things to offer. We are a rich tapestry of threads and colors. Together we are a beautiful fabric. Do you believe you are unique and special? You are able to do and be certain things that I am never able to. That is great. Enjoy what you can do and do it with all your heart.

I love to write—I am thankful that I am finally at the place where I can be productive and it is a release that helps me to live in the world. I take in too much information and can get too stimulated and I release the pressure through writing. It is my special task that causes my whole life to fall into place. I am a better husband and neighbor and friend because I write. It is who I am. Who are you and what do you need to be doing?

What a bizarre, cool thing to believe, without a shadow of a doubt, that you are Buddha or Christ or Satan. It is frightening and can be liberating. I would think that it would open some doors into acting ability. I know it helps me in writing characters and letting them go on their own to act out their dialogue and deed. I can trust them.

Can we trust our delusions? Sometimes I could and I found it comforting to be back with the common theme. In early psychosis I usually had a compulsion to in-line skate across the country for mental health awareness. I told this to the last guy that I bought a pair of blades from. He happened to have worked with bipolar people in the past and he just went with the flow. It felt good to have someone on my side—he helped me with a payment plan and I bought the skates and trained for the pursuit. Perhaps if I had involved the correct people the event would have occurred. It always died as I slipped into my post manic depression and then it would rise again the next manic phase.

Your delusions of grandeur can disturb you. That is a good thing— it shows that you are sane and struggling with your real self to sort out the insane in you. It can be a strange and surreal pursuit and fight.

Your delusions are part of your illness and, in a way, part of you. They were and are real; our internal world assimilated the delusions as whole realities. But how do we heal and let them go? We need to address them as reality, we need to react to them with emotion and figure them out. (reference #1) Sometimes there is not much to figure out. I don't think we can fully move on until we accept and deal with them as actually happening to us.

Maybe part of you needs to grieve their loss. They can be like our friends. They can be the healthiest self-esteem we have lived in a long time. Is there any good we can take from them as we move on? Are you holding on to your delusions of grandeur for any reasons? Is everyone in your family a high achiever and this is the way that you can keep up in your sub-conscious? We are complicated beings.

Delusions of grandeur are a strange component of this manic psychosis. We must be able to accept them as really happening and forgive ourselves and work through them. We, again, have much personal responsibility to accept. Personally, I don't miss this feature very often. Delusions can be hard on the head; though I fully believe that they are helping me in the gift side to be open to full possibilities. It has blown the doors of my old limited self. I am a new person capable of new things. Memories of my delusions of grandeur help me through the hundreds of rejections I have received in submitting my writing. I always improve my writing and sometimes I can learn from what they say. At other times I accept that they are simply at the wrong address. My creations are looking for the right people at the right address.

I still get slight wanderings in this grandiose direction and I try to accept them and focus on where I am and what I need. I find that the grandeur places can be an escape but I don't want to avoid my life anymore—it is becoming too good to miss any. Sometimes my delusions of grandeur go away on their own and sometimes the larger ones need medicine to eradicate them. Talk to your doctor.

My delusions of grandeur were not big on action—they tended to talk and think a lot. And few others were appreciative of my special place or abilities. There can be a fine line between delusions of grandeur and a healthy dose of anything-is-possible self-esteem. I know that for me to pursue the reality of writing full time for money, I need to think big. My old grandeur experiences help me believe in getting there. I just don't live it out in my head though. I persevere to develop my craft and style. No one else can do it for me—it takes work.

I hope that you can leave delusions of grandeur in the past, yet dig into the possibility—you can do great things that nobody else can do. One of the tricky spots to overcome in my psychosis was the early stage where everything was incredible and beautiful. I would always get overwhelmed with the big ideas and flop to a stop, and roll around in the illness of psychosis.

Perhaps it was a form of training to deal with the big events in life and what goes on in my head. I did become much better at managing the situation so that I wasn't overwhelmed. It was key for me to not be freaked out by what is going on. Stay cool and relaxed and follow your sheet of paper for what to do in the situation. Did you write a balance prompt sheet of actions for yourself?

You can get through this with the help of your support network and your doctor and your own head. Give yourself credit and believe. I know you can do it.

Points of thought and action:

#1 How have I experienced delusions of grandeur?

#2 What prevents or slows down or arrests this grandeur thinking?

#3 Have I emotionally embraced the reality of my experiences with delusions of grandeur?

#4 What does my cheat sheet / prompt list tell me to do when deluded with grandeur?

#5 Can I still dream of my ideal life?

#6 (My personal plan.)

SELF-PITY

I am now in the midst of self-pity. I hate it. I have this condition of the inner ear where fragments are dislodged and accumulate and it results in vertigo and nausea and hallucinations of movement.

I went to the doctor yesterday and he was confident of the diagnosis and communicated a simple series of movements as the main treatment to shake up the accumulation. I woke up this morning spinning in bed, my body covered in sweat; wanting to puke. I stayed still in bed for another few hours. This, in combination with the lack of sunshine in the last month, could send me into depression. I have to learn to deal with it.

I'm afraid to move at times and these exercises make it worse sometimes before making it better. I am just starting to learn to deal with it. The other night I kicked the bed like a little kid: make it stop please. I spin fast forward, sideways, and backwards simultaneously. Did I mention that I hate it? I am feeling sorry for myself.

I am attempting to see the good in feeling sorry for myself: I want and need to get better. My system recognizes this thing as unwanted and unneeded. Are you telling me I need to live with this always? I can't accept that right now. I want to baby myself. Please make it go away, make it go away Mommy, fix it, I don't need this, wa, wa, wa. Will it ever end?

I need to approach those nasty exercises soon and see if this is one of the times that it will make it better. My doctor was rather rushed in seeing me yesterday: therefore I do not know all that I should. He gave me a copy of one of his textbook pages and it does not explain how to approach the exercise. But there are handwritten notes on three drugs to prescribe—funny how that works.

I will get through this like everything else. I will die someday and I want to feel great and enjoy life till that day. Attitude is everything. I will allow myself a little time to grieve the acceptance of this condition. I don't want to deal with it. Take it away, please and thank you.

I think it can be a human ego stroke to make a diagnosis. The doctor said to me yesterday that I had diagnosed it properly as the inner ear. I felt a wave of pride over my self-diagnosis. Do doctors enjoy the categorizing? As a kid I watched Sesame Street, and played "Which one of these ones is not like the other?" I loved to make that call. Which is the same and which is different?

So we have a genuine medical condition. It is diagnosed and it makes sense and in some cases we have a second opinion. We naturally rebel at the notion of this illness. This is a great trait: who wants an illness? Some people do, but that is another matter. I felt sorry for myself and grieved the loss of health and balance.

I have to go to an extreme of denial before coming back to accept the condition. I never want to own the limitations and the medical prophecies—they have been known to be wrong. I believe in the power of suggestion and self-fulfilled prophecy. Denial in the long run will be where you live—we make the choices to limit ourselves. The doctor or textbook does not define us.

It is good, and natural, to feel self-pity. If you never work through it and move on it is a bad thing. These conditions of health can be serious and it is good that our emotions take them seriously. I want to baby myself back to not having this situation. I do not want to accept it. If I feel sorry for myself it will make me feel better. I will disappear into a wallow of self.

In the grand scheme of things, my vertigo is nothing. I am alive and warm and fed. Who am I to whine about such a condition?

You could say these things about bipolar. When bipolar jolts, you can have a hard time finding volunteers to trade illnesses with you. There's nothing good to be seen in it. But we must. We must crawl out of our desperate hole of self-affliction one step at a time. Nobody else can do it. We must take those steps. I don't even know what to do yet to overcome this sick feeling of vertigo. I have to research and talk to people and experiment—just like with bipolar.

Well, I psyched myself up to try the exercises. To the right once and I flew into an awful spin and twist, to the center, grabbed the puke bucket and went over to the left and vomited immediately. I went up to center and could not face doing anymore. I rested and did the movement just with the head—and vomited to the end of my stomach. That is a hard treatment to face. The research is growing. There is a homeopathic remedy that helps people with the condition and we found out about other exercises.

I still hate this but I have to move through it somehow. It helped me write this chapter to have a fresh dose of self-pity. I will get there somehow. Did I say that I hate it? I will surmount and overcome and learn to limit the bad aspects and live with it. I have overcome many other things and this is just another one to face down. Because I have faced the bipolar challenge it is second nature to get through obstacles.

I learned that this benign paroxysmal positional vertigo could be caused in part by my back flip, landing on my head, when I was psychotic. Debris moves around to cause accumulations and nerve sensation triggering. Does it make me feel bad that I may have caused it? Today is a good day and I am grasping onto some solutions, hopefully these exercises eliminate the symptoms. I had a long but restful night propped up on pillows. I am concentrating on soaking up some sunshine and gaining a triumphant attitude.

What amazes me always about illness is the reminder it offers to enjoy your life and be grateful for the good times. Give thanks for what goodness you do have and make it grow. Make a list of things you need to be thankful for and focus on it daily, hourly and by the minute. Tap into your dreaming ability and focus on that. Take small steps toward your dream. It will be hard, yet if you pursue your desires, assistance will come in both easily-spotted and disguised ways. We have to change our thinking to overcome self-pity. As long as we focus on the rot of pity, we will erode. As someone said, "I was upset that I had no shoes till I met a man that had no legs."

Self-pity is part of dealing with a situation. Ideally it is a phase and it will pass. The sun will come out again and someday you will see good things about your condition. We are adaptable creatures and things do not feel right immediately; but, with time, the weirdest thing can be an old friend. We need to plug into this adaptable tendency to leave the illness side of bipolar and enter the gift.

If I can do it, you can too. You will soon be in the place where others pity you and you are leaving pity behind. You are moving away from the bad sides of illness and learning who you are, including your self-pity aspects. We each have unique patterns of self-pity that can be hooked up to our experiences in growing up. I just want my wife to baby me now and make me feel good. Living with bipolar we need to baby ourselves sometimes. The trick is to know when and for how long. Soon others will forget to pity us or even ask us about the bipolar tendency.

In drug rehabilitation I had a wonderful counselor named Doris who would pass us a pity chamber pot if we were having a pity party. I liked this. It helped us to move on from feeling sorry for ourselves and to build concrete bridge improvements for not dwelling on the past. We could not even talk in a self-pitying manner: we were conditioned to speak in new ways or to say nothing. We changed our language of thought. This is a tough and effective solution.

If you are feeling self-pity there is most likely an underlying reason. You must explore this and learn about yourself. If a person is living just in the illness perspective of bipolar it is a given that you should feel empathy—it is a terrible place. You don't want to stay there. But you have to accept a condition before you can move on from it. You can leave the ill effects of bipolar behind and break through.

You can do it with the right attitude and approach of honesty and courage. I wish you plenty of courage to face what bipolar throws at you.

Points of thought and action:
#1   Do I feel self-pity?
#2   Have I grieved my self-pity?
#3   Have I had my time in denial?
#4   Have I pampered myself?
#5   Have I kicked myself to new ways of thinking and action?
#6   (My personal plan.)

SUPPORT NETWORK

We need to reach outside of our thinking and beyond our significant other and our family to a support network; then we can live our life to its richest and most balanced.

We used to be more dependent on one another for survival: for food, protection and warmth. With progress, in a consumer society, we cocoon in our own little worlds. These self-contained domiciles can be lonely and sad places. We surf the net, watch our TVs and listen to our radios and they inform us that happiness is in our next purchase. We buy that item and bring it home to our place and it shines for a moment. And if we do not have much money, it makes us feel inadequate.

We each have different social needs. They can be influenced by the way you were raised as to the number of people you need around you. I believe we each have ideal ratios of togetherness: a certain amount of your time you need to be by yourself, with your lover, your family, one on one, in a group, and out in public. You can list your own categories involved in your social life. The main thing is for you to be aware of your ideal social situation—and know it changes with age, pursuit, and bipolar.

Pets can be part of our family. It can be easier to communicate with your pet than with people. Katie, our cat has taught me about unconditional love and forgiveness. She accepts and gives to me in my bad times. I have learned about instinct and natural tendency. It can be useful to get out of ourselves and live for someone else. This can include a pet. We have to feed and care for someone other than our self.

Katie picks up on my moods and intensities and it is an extra warning light for me to care for my needs. I find it more of a wake up call to see her suffer because of my intensities. Back in my not being able to sleep days, entering psychosis, I had trouble with pets barking and wanting to cuddle and bug me. Sometimes it can be a challenge to be around an animal. Yet pets can be beneficial to our health. They can accept us and cuddle with us and bring out our best.

A support network will catch us if we fall. Your network can consist of any number of people. They can include your doctor and counselor, your spiritual advisor, and your bowling friend. You need your own group. The important thing is to start involving them in your bipolar recovery and gift seeking. They will be invaluable as you move to a fuller life.

Since I have been writing I spend more time by myself and in nature. Writing is a form of social structure in my head. I still desperately need other people: my wife, my family, and my friends. I need to be in public just to watch people—it keeps me balanced.

Bipolar challenges our social world—it can alienate everyone that we know. We can find ourselves all alone. Everyone could be reaching out to us but still there is no contact—we are ill, and our illness can be a place where no one can reach. There is a beautiful Robin Williams movie, *What Dreams May Come.* It is an amazing, mental torment portrayal of the distance from your loved ones. It is a place where few are able to visit.

As ill bipolar people we need to lighten up and try to be easier on our friends and family. They are occasionally heroes in not abandoning us. I was challenging, and am thankful that people stuck by me. Give thanks if you have people that love you. Cherish them.

To have friends you must be a friend. If you want someone to listen to you, try listening to them. One method of befriending someone is to get them talking and ask them questions and listen; be interested and they will tend to like you. Most people love to talk about themselves and their interests. You can disclose some of your life to them and this will draw you together. They will tend to want to share some of their life with you. Some people are incapable of hearing certain things and we need to be aware of these limitations. Ultimately in our support network we need to make people aware of our changing situation, and then they are more capable of support and encouragement.

It can take years to develop friendships with certain people. And you can be fast friends with others in a day. Some of us experience few social blocks. I enjoyed the camaraderie of my hospitalized days—talk about a quick connection with people. These people are great phone numbers to have—call them when you get out and talk about your feelings of being institutionalized, few others will understand how ingrained the institution is within you.

I found it best to have many people to talk with. It is great if you have a family member who takes an interest in being supportive to you. It can be as simple as talking for a few minutes or setting up an agreement with them: if you behave in a certain way they will take you to see your doctor. It is up to you as far as what you need. You could write out agreed-upon contracts that they can show you to get you to look after yourself.

We, as bipolar people, change more than other people do and this can be a strain on our friendships. We need to be easy on them and not burn one person out. Develop your own stress busters like journaling and exercise—you will be able to give your people more if you know how to look after yourself. Be friendly—develop a good attitude and you will make friends as you need them.

I could chart my mood by the number of social contacts I have in a day. When I was depressed I liked to pull away from everyone and become a recluse—I had nothing to offer and could not relate to people. When I was hypo and entering the first stages of mania I was a social animal—I needed to bounce off of people and I could not resist interaction. Now I find myself in-between and the best part is I am able to consciously make choices to go in either direction. I can ramp up my social ability to interact. I have developed the skills. It is not always easy but I can make the choice and do it. And I can tone down the contacts and pull away. I need both directions at times.

If I am a little down, an interaction with a stranger or a friend can set me in a better head space. If I am getting a little spun out, I can pull away from people and digest the stimulus. My social contacts directly influence my balance.

In my hospitalizations, during the admission interview, I started my debriefing. I trusted and used the staff's confidence. Upon admittance, I whirled in a psychotic tendency and I found that by talking to them about the details I could remember, I had a method of coming down. We cannot keep this psychosis inside us. Use your writing or art or hobbies as a release but please develop people that you can talk to. You are not the only one who experiences these things—confess your deeds to someone. Not everyone can handle it; therefore if you can, choose your confidants. Even write your confession down and then burn it in a safe manner: this can be a step toward health.

The nurse's job is to portray normal behavior to us—we can trust a nurse to be a good sounding board. If they have been around for a while they have heard it all. Talk to your doctor, he or she is your key to freedom from the hospital and illness. We have to learn to communicate within ourselves to be honest about our experiences. Our addictive side can be a smooth talker. What do we need to achieve better balance? This is a vital form of communication—you need to always be comparing your present self with your ideal balance.

There are times when you need to avoid certain people. They are upset and it will do you no good to try to help them. Sometimes you are able to be strong enough to assist them but at other times you cannot do anything to help them. Do you know when you can be with certain people and when you need to be far away?

I am sensitive to others and their moods and attitudes. Even in public with total strangers I choose to avoid certain people, they project anger and fear or violence. They can suck you into their stew—we have to be aware to avoid these pitfalls. We can build social protections but there are times when you need to just step away from that person—he or she is not for you. It will do neither of you any good to interact. I will not ruin my good feeling by getting upset with you over a delay in a line-up: delays can be a nice chance to take in the world from a different perspective.

We have to become experts at interacting. We have many potential problems to work through. We may not even be aware of who we are. This illness can screw us around big time. We may be so accustomed to having to act from depression, we play ourselves like a marionette. When we do start to live healthier lives—this is one thing we struggle with. How do we present our true selves? And people may not be ready or capable of knowing our truth. Like all that we face, the more work we put into it this year, the easier it will be the next year.

My people-pleasing tendency still affects me more than I want it to. I think that the world revolves around me, but I need to please this person and be on his or her good side. That is a mixed state. Depending on my health and strength I can have a hard time distinguishing if something is my problem or the other person's. Do I choose to fight this battle?

I tend to want to change the world to be a better place. But there is no getting around the fact that this person I need to work with for a few weeks is a total jerk, period. I need to get the job done and interact professionally and stay away otherwise. It is the other person's problem—nobody else likes this person, so why should I make the effort? Just stay away, and it will be over soon enough, maybe you will never see this person again, and, if so, give thanks. But if I am tired and not doing well I may have real trouble with thinking it is my problem and fault. There are many people who never have to deal with these internal dramatics.

What do you have to deal with in your internal world that affects your social outcome? Do you need to work on your social skills? How we interact with the world can help or hinder us. How we communicate with a doctor will affect his or her decisions about our responsibility capabilities. If we want empowerment we need to communicate responsibly. What do you want from life?

We bipolar people have needs to have community around us that we can communicate with. You could even have an actual organized support group—that is great. But I trust that your group leads you from the illness toward the gifting of bipolar. Are you being encouraged to deal with your problems and to eventually move on?

It is great to talk and to be heard and to listen. I have found groups to be useful yet I have not used them much. I tend to not like listening to people moan and whine about their situations. I don't want to hear the same problem over and over again with no results. I want to hear that you are dealing with your life concerns. For me it depends on who is facilitating to decide whether it is good or not. We need to use groups to be empowered to decrease our illness traits and not just whine about problems forever. This approach of complaining can actually be detrimental to your health. We have to change the past by changing the way we think and talk about it. Our present reality will be transformed.

We need to teach responsibility and to take our empowerment seriously. We each have the power to change our lives—the biggest effect, quite often, is in our attitudes. You can hear much about someone's attitude in the way he or she converses. My life is too short to listen to someone stuck in one place, moaning about his or her poor life.

Life can suck—people have horrible situations. Your life may be terrible. But it can be different. I have met people who should not be happy, or alive, after what they've been through. But they are full of joy. Why is that? Can you be happy? Can you choose joy and contentment? I believe that you can take small steps in that direction. Momentum will build and you will be surprised someday when you are happy with your life.

You may need to join a group, or change groups. You might need to stop going to group. Your situation is yours and you can change your life for the better. Make a new friend. You can do it. You can face that group and attend and be honest. Perhaps you have been unable to be truthful about your situation for years. It can take time to break these deception walls down.

We need to be able to de-brief and counsel with people we trust. It is up to you to build your friends into who you need. Some people are not capable of providing support to us in our illness stages. You may need to move on from certain friends if they are not good for you. And then there are others who are left behind as we move from our illness into our gift—we lose them because they are not able to move on from a care-giver role. They need you in a down, needy place where they can help you and be comfortable.

We need to be aware of our relationships and how they change. We need different friends at different times. You may need a soft shoulder to cry on and then, next month, you need someone to follow through with a point of intervention. Perhaps you have credit card issues—you could set up with a trusted friend to hold your credit card during that certain period when you are in your manic spending tendency.

It can be tricky to build trust in people to manage your money; we cannot trust ourselves in certain states so we need to trust other people. Perhaps we need zero access to our money and a simple allowance from our financial advisor person. He or she will make sure our bills are paid. Our very lives can depend on other people. You can gain independence again in the future. We need to make the best of interdependence.

This subject of friends and support is, again, your responsibility. I do not accept self-pity in this department. We as bipolar people have abilities to make friends—we can do it better than non-bipolar people.

Our social hang-ups have been blown away in times of social butterfly mania: tap back into that verve to approach people.

We have empathy and humor and sensitivity to interact with people: people like to hang out with us. And we may have to go through more trial friends to find the ones that fit with us. Not everyone can handle our situations.

I went to Cuba by myself to counter the long winter and my pattern of mania. I stepped from the plane and found myself rising in mania. I was partially aware from practice. I had no choice but to build a temporary network with total strangers for that two-week period. I needed someone to talk to. I smiled and was nice and talked to people. I asked them questions and listened. I told them a bit about myself and my plan to deal with the mania by avoiding the length of winter in Canada. I think people responded better because they were in holiday mode and things like this did not bother them as much as if I were near their home.

People accepted me and hoped the best for me. I disappeared for a couple of days in psychosis, and when I re-appeared, it helped to have people concerned. People were accepting and fun and peaceful—it helped me to focus on good things and leave the mess of my head behind.

When we climbed on the bus to get to the airport I had a little rage episode concerning money for the bus. I had spent all my money and I thought that the bus was included. People calmed me down and told me I had worked hard to get through this and to not let a little thing throw me off. It was great that these new friends helped me out—I think someone paid my way. I have never seen them again and that is okay. It is wonderful to help people and to be helped.

That is one aspect of bipolar that has left a legacy—it forced me to be dependent on others when I was younger and forged me into a member of a community. I needed help and had to learn to accept it. This bipolar forces us to deal with our pride of independence. I am a better person for having the skills to work with other people—I can compromise and debate and meet them where they are. I can sell people on an idea and use tact and diplomacy—bipolar has enhanced these skills. What has it enhanced in you?

It has developed in me the ability to make connections with people—I pick up on details of their life and can bridge to them. I can depend on people and delegate.

Having said all of this my wife and I have moved a few times in the last four years and we have friends spread out all over the place. It would be nice to have a few more where we live and this is something we are working on. I find it is a challenge to find couples that we can both hang out with and enjoy. It seems like we need several more contacts and acquaintances to have enough. You cannot have a meaningful relationship with everyone, but you have your needs for social contact. Our world gets busier and it seems like many people are too busy—we need to let this go and focus on our good friendships.

What good is a gift if you have no one to share it with? Part of living full life with bipolar is being yourself to enjoy friends. This is a great part of life. This is part of the gift. Your social needs are different now as a bipolar person. You may need more or less time alone. You will come to know yourself deeper and better and you will choose the best ways to live your life.

You will have the best friends and support people by being open and willing to invest in building these unions—yet know when to cut your losses. Some people will jeopardize your health and life. We have limited time. Who will you choose to spend time with?

Our friends and family can be our lifeline if we empower them to be. They can remind us of who we are in sanity—and they can be our template for leaving insanity and regaining our lives. They can know us deeply and help us to live. We can help them optimize their happiness and joy. One of the potential risks and advantages of living close with a bipolar person is you will be challenged to know yourself in a deeper way. We will challenge you in a way that few others will. I ask people questions they are unaccustomed to answering. I like to challenge myself to better thinking and deeds and I like to push other people as well.

What are your special gifts and challenges in this social area? People can be alienated and attracted by bipolar. It is a paradox that we have to live with. We are gifted to live enhanced.

Your support network is yours to create and enhance and use. Have fun with your life and your loved ones. This is part of the icing of life. Enjoy.

Points of thought and action:

#1   Do I have a support network? Do I need a formal group?

#2   Who can I talk to about certain subjects?

#3   What do I deal with internally that affects my social world?

#4   How do I need to treat and use my support network to better my bipolar?

#5   How can I look after myself better to give to my network?

#6   (My personal plan.)

PRIDE

There is good pride and bad pride and it is certain that bipolar will take you for a ride in one or both of these departments. Delusions of grandeur can make you feel better than everyone. How are you recovering from this? Has depression raked you over the fiery barbs to make you feel worthless?

Do you judge yourself for being bipolar? We need to come through to the point of acceptance—we need to get past the anger and denial and guilt. You did nothing wrong to get this condition. Even if there was a connection to your actions, so what? Does it do anyone any good to play the name game? I took street drugs before my onset of bipolar—did my actions contribute to the illness? Does it matter what I did in the past if I take responsibility for my actions? I can seek forgiveness, restitution, and health. The best thing I can do is to not take street drugs anymore and feel good about it.

I believe that bipolar can blow us up to taste a bit of the whole human experience. The full range—you name it and bipolar has given me a taste, and at a quick pace. How you turn this into good in your life will be unique. I could spend my lifetime writing the experiences I have had. The tough part, to begin with, is to survive the ride and then slow it down to take some control back. We will and do take control. In our bipolar illness days, we may be feared and judged and looked down upon, but we will learn to let it go and not care about what others say—we will move on from them. We will lose our people-pleasing traits—this, too, is pride.

We need to arrive at the place of being proud of taming the bipolar beast. This can help balance the stigma teardown. You are amazing to receive the grace to even attempt this taming, let alone succeed. Wow. We have the power to change our lives for good. We can earn pride in our control of the illness side. We should feel great about stopping a mania or depression in its tracks. To be proactive is something to be proud of. You are doing great. But don't get too big a head—I found mine always exploded and I had to rebuild again.

We are working through the negative. We are achieving more than surviving it. It may take us one year or twenty years but we will get there. We need to be proud of what this illness has provided for us. It has changed us into better persons of possibility. We are new creatures. Bipolar can teach us to listen and be sensitive to small details of situation and people. We can develop great emotional intelligence in relating to where people are. We have dragged hell and soared the heavens; we can interact with people emotionally where they are. We have felt the shame of self. We have felt on top of the world and can celebrate with the best of them.

We will be in harmony with our world and our internal self. Our pride will be in balance. We will not be fearful of looking bad—this too is pride. We cannot control our reputation—too much about a reputation is controlled by other people's subjective experience judging us. We can control how we think, act, feel and treat people: this will enhance our reputation. We will not care how we appear in leaving the illness and tapping into the gift. We will try things and not have our whole person affected by how other people react. We can get on stage if we want and need to. We can play music and act and speak. We can do anything that we dream and work for. The world will help us out.

We will live as only we can to enhance our world. People will appreciate us for who we are. We are unique lovely creatures. We need to kill that manic within us that is superior and arrogant. Bipolar can enhance us to have more skill sets. I feel bad for some so called normal people who are afraid to live life—bipolar has forced me to take risks and I enjoy more of life because of this.

We have the gift to focus intensely to the point of delusion on something we need—we can tune out reality if we want, if we decide it is okay with no damage being done. We can then focus fully on our task or thoughts with exclusion of all else. This is a huge advantage to make progress in your chosen pursuits and ideas. You can tap into that intensity to get your work done, but be careful to just do it for periods of time and look after yourself and your relationships.

Keep it up; you have worked hard to get to this point and it will get easier and other things will get harder, but you will work it through; and breakthroughs will continue to arrive. When you deal with a section of your life, you gain momentum to face down the next challenge that much quicker.

Like the addiction support groups, we need to perform a fearless moral inventory of ourselves. We need to celebrate our good and great points and we need to forgive, forget, and improve on some of our negative points. Can you hold your head up high with your regrets? Talk to your people and research your atonement—accept your true self with love. Love yourself as your neighbor. The bible says, "Love your neighbor as yourself."

Desire points of change to remedy the bad. You can make a difference in how you feel. Does depression, or procrastination, have you paralyzed? Do you spin your wheels in the same little box? Can you just not go for that very thing that is calling you? Your whole life waits for you patiently—the universe wants to line up to help you. You have to change your thoughts and actions. Bipolar can torture us into paralysis. We need to accept periods in our life where we are capable of nothing. To do nothing is extremely positive when you consider the suicidal option. There are many urges with bipolar to walk in dark deeds. How do we change our actions? Make plans ahead of time, like your prompt lists, for when you are depressed or manic or in mixed states. If you feel an urge you really don't want to obey, do something else. We have to retrain our mind to take detours in our pre-wired thinking. The next chapter talks about the recordings we play in our head—this is vital to live our lives effectively and not be controlled in undesirable ways.

Pride is a tough balance to achieve. It takes practice and study. It is worth having the confidence in yourself to achieve, yet it is best not to be high on your self. Vanity is ugly. We need to let go of delusions of grandeur yet hold onto the tenacity to rise above the illness—we can be wonderfully gifted people who possess unique abilities. That is something to be proud of. And with this we will counter the misinformation of stigma. We will get to the place of pride with this bipolar. We do have an advantage, a challenging enhancement to live fuller lives. We can do it and leave the world a better place.

We can be heroes. You are a hero if you haven't killed yourself. You are my hero to face bipolar down—you are amazing to get into this book. Many people are not ready for responsibility, but you are leaving your illness behind. You are taking control of your thoughts and actions and emotions. Sure, you still get taken for the odd ride now and then, but that's all right, we're human.

Great work—you are amazing. Imagine what you can do and live and see. Feel it, do it.

Points of thought and action:

#1　How does depression and mania affect my pride and life?

#2　What are my good and bad traits?

#3　What are my priorities and values?

#4　How can I let go of other people judging me? Even if it is just playing out in my mind?

#5　How can I feel solid about myself?

#6　(My personal plan.)

RECORDINGS WE PLAY

We all play or replay certain tracks of audio coaching in our heads from time to time—it is an automatic feature in many of us. We may not even be aware of whom or what triggers our self-talk. We enter the loop: it could be our parents or someone from our youth that recites this spiel in our head. Over and over it plays with no exception and steals us from where we are.

It can claim our ability to be engaged in our life. And it is a different tape for each of us. We can compose the content ourselves or receive it all from others. What tapes do you play? What loops of thought do you repeat to no gain? Do they keep you down? Are you aware of the loops that you fall into? Does making a mistake, even the smallest one, throw you into a funk of self-reproach? You go into your self-loathing, 'you're good for nothing' speech; you go on for minutes and into hours. It takes you for a ride—you lose control and time.

If you have not become aware of this trend and taken action to retrain your mind, these speech loops of thought will most likely have negative effects on you. They can freeze your situation to extend its time in reality; and the more we spend in a certain reality, the more we will tend to dwell there. We need to break down these frequent treadmills of repeated thought and emotion. We need to create fresh places to dwell in. We want to feel good.

You may be fortunate to have positive tapes that you play—you are blessed and are a few steps ahead of the rest of us. You may have had a coach when you were younger that would yell encouragement, "You can do it, dig deep, go!" You can pull this out when things are tough for you and play it to enhance and build on.

We need to be responsible for our thoughts—they tend to turn into action and emotions. Thoughts, actions, and emotions tend to revolve and manifest themselves. Which come first? Each can affect the other. We can change our thinking through reading and planned ways of thinking. We can even decide to change how we feel.

You can make notes of how you want to think in certain situations. Perhaps when you face your doctor you are frightened. It takes you back to your father figure and you have fear of your doctor. You become aware of this and you decide to work with your counselor to make a thought plan for yourself. You don't want to switch doctors yet and you want to face this situation. You write down a paragraph of affirmation concerning your approach to meeting your doctor. You read it over and over again while you wait to see him. You burn a new way of thinking into your head—we can change our thinking patterns. You might decide to talk to the doctor about it.

By changing our thinking we can change our actions—we can choose to do things that will help and not hinder us. We can take away the power of the automatic pilot to drink alcohol—we can choose to go to a support meeting and deal with our Hungry, Angry, Lonely, and Tired; we can halt our need to drink. We can take back control of our actions and emotions. Every time we decide to do something good for our health, we gain power and positive emotion. This is a personal war with you acting as opposing generals. Think about it. Aren't you your worst enemy? You may say it is other people who screw with your life, but isn't it you giving them that ability for negative in your life?

You possess the ultimate power to command your battleground. When I was ill, there was no doubt that my life was a battleground. I could not accept the casualty of my death; I learned, and practiced giving more power to my good general. After a decade of war, I left the battlefield and entered the arena. I play my life out in a safer place now: my life is no longer in danger. The good general won. Give your good general new tapes to play to gain power.

You can compose your own thought tracks to counter the negative thoughts that you fall into. Do you hear your parents, grandparents, siblings, and friends in your head? Is what they're saying good for you? You can shut them up and give them new things to say, it is your head. You don't have to be a 'do what they say' person. Don't allow them the control over your thoughts, actions, and emotions. Take responsibility for your thinking. Clean house. Memorize positive passages of spiritual text or poetry: absorb goodness and let your thoughts marinate. The sweet flavor will play out in your life.

We need to identify the negative tapes we play—this can take years. Write it down, there can be keywords. "Going down, I'm going down, to the depths, it's where I belong…" Down could be a key word for this spiel. I write it down and counter it with whatever works, it will take many tries to perfect it. "Down, down, up, up, balance, make a net, set it up to catch the fall, I'm not going there, I will medicate and walk and talk and sleep and be good to myself…" This may come out sounding goofy but please realize the power you have to control every word you think about and say in your brain. And you need to learn to do it on the spot when your thoughts turn on you—you can take responsibility for your thoughts.

When you record your voice to counter your themes of negative, you could have your inspirational music in the background. You could listen to it when you walk and face down your tough situations—you could listen to it in bed each night. It is your head and it can take you for rides, you do not have to sit in the back seat, you can cut the engine. You can stop your patterns of thinking and behavior and emotions. You have the power and choice—there are no excuses. Certain jobs like sales thrive in this area. Talk to a salesperson about their head talk and self-coaching and most likely they will be able to give you some tips.

We can choose to jump into our emotions straight ahead and change the way we feel. We can decide whether to react in a certain way or not. Someone cuts us off in the car and we can let it go. We can think about where we are going and how good it will be. I find this a hard one to counter at times—when people endanger my life in a vehicle. It upsets me but I strive to let it go, it does me no good to carry that person with me through the day.

The themes we play in our head are crucial to our emotional well-being. The bible talks about renewing your mind. I believe what you think about, you will become. I strive to think like a writer and choose to be positive about my style and craft—but it can be hard to maintain this headset. I make conscious choices to dwell in the good place I want to be. I want to be a full time writer who makes great money and makes a difference in mental health. It feels good to imagine being there now. It attracts more good and the bad dissipates.

It takes constant vigilance to counter the tracks in your head. When I was in drug rehabilitation, one of the exercises in our small group was to tape a piece of paper on our backs that had a poem, *Who I am.* These new friends wrote things on my back that blew me away. I had no clue as to who I was. We had beaten ourselves up to a bad place of pride—we doubted, but enough of a glimmer shone through to me. Later, the opportunity came to review and to build upon these facts that others had observed.

Do you know what great traits you possess? Do you know one good thing about you? You can ask others if you need to. Write down a list and build on it. You are a unique person who needs to know yourself. Make a list. Learn how you can enhance these gifts. Play the tape of who you are over and over. It is true. Bipolar will shake our personality and awareness to shreds—we need to counter and build from a solid foundation of facts. We are good people that are… Play it over and over again.

Listen to audio from the library—a variety of subjects are there to strengthen you. Make personalized audio for yourself. Remember your personal triumphs and celebrate and review and build on them. "I made the choice to leave that job and I haven't looked back since." "I asked him out for that date and he said yes and we are happily together now." "I went for a walk." "I said no to that drink." "I said yes to taking a risk and stepping toward my dream." "I tried." "I forgave myself." Remember, and celebrate your wonderful attributes and life experiences—this will be your fertile garden for more of the same. Create your new head to live your fresh life.

Bipolar affects every aspect of our life yet we need to tame it to where we need to go. It can take us over and we can whimper at every whim it commands. It can control us or we can control it. It is our choice. It starts in our head and requires much discipline and desire. Do you want to get better? You need to strive to make changes in your thinking and actions and emotion. You have more power than you realize.

You can condition your thinking to build in warning lights and alarms. One that I built in was my loss of sleep—if I lose one night of sleep the alarms go off in my head and I take actions to guard the next night's sleep. It sounds so simple yet in the midst of the action of hypo or mania it can seem like a great thing to not have to sleep and all is a wonderful adventure. I had to build in a system to get some sleep or it became breakup time and I would lose months of my life. I had to learn to counter my illness traits, to build protections so I would not blow all my money on manic spending. I chose to resist opening my sexual addiction door. I had to play different tapes when my thinking blurred and twisted psychotic. I had to take my medication.

Did you see the movie *A Beautiful Mind*? If you deal with psychosis I would watch this movie as part of your training. You will see a textbook approach to dealing with your delusions: he accepts their presence and chooses to not encourage them, he focuses elsewhere and his delusional characters tend to slide into the background. You can do this too and you will learn your own special approaches.

We need to be open-minded to build a resistance with many options and possibilities. Music can soothe, energize and empower. Movies can help us. I had been dealing with this inner ear situation and I was finding myself to be a chicken with a bad attitude. I watched a couple of war movies that set my priorities straight to give thanks and dwell in gratitude and courage.

Be open to self-help concepts—who else will help you as much as you can or will? You have to study and build motivation. Check out some motivational speakers. Like everything take what works for you and leave the rest. Sometimes we have no idea what will work for us until we try. Cultivating a mind of possibility to reach your gift is essential. The smallest item of learning can combine with others to counter your major extremes.

We have to build a resistance working with everything we have. You know what areas you need to build up: it could be your support group, your doctor, your resistance to addictions; you have to wage war on that weak part of your self. You can eliminate, strengthen, and transform your internal world of thinking. Help is all around you if you open your heart with attitude. A singing bird can be your cheerleader; a child that smiles at you can heal your day. This is your day of life to live well. Paint your canvas daily.

You have to be an athlete of the mind to leave the illness of bipolar and live in the gift. It can take many years to get there but what is the alternative? You are where you are and that will not change for the better without your cooperation. We have to work at getting better. Do something inspirational. Listen to music. Watch a *Rocky* movie. Challenge your thinking to include health. You can let go of the illness model. Whatever you focus on with your thoughts, actions, and emotions will grow.

What are you growing in your garden? You can pull your weeds and grow great fruit. Don't listen to people who limit you. What right has a doctor to say—after one or two psychotic episodes—that you will be on anti psychotic tranquilizers for your life? I will take small steps toward where I want to be. I will not listen to anyone who tells me that I cannot do something. I will listen to what you have to say and learn from it but I am a believer in triumph and possibility through adversity. You have no right to tell me my life will be this way or that. I can change my life to what I want to live. I will not accept this illness, I will try and try and slide back and fall and get back up and strive and talk and walk and learn and struggle to live.

It is worth the fight and I am glad there is no easy solution—it is harder that way; a pill alone will not cure me, it will help but it is tough to get into the gift of bipolar. Can you do it? I did and you can too. Are you hungry? Victory tastes great.

In the arena where this illness can affect us most, in our minds and thinking, we need to rise up in rebellion and stage a coup. We need to rise up against these thoughts of mania and depression, we need to medicate and be honest with ourselves. It takes practice and discipline but we can do it with help.

It is your choice to make thousands of choices in your next month to improve your life and existence. It is up to you. How will you choose? And if you make a bad choice will you chastise your self and play that loop of self-hate or will you learn from your mistake to be aware and maybe not make the same mistake next time? How do you react to your mistakes? They can be the greatest guide to the path you need to tread, or you can wallow in the ditch and play that negative loop over and over—your choice. Trial and error is how I approached bipolar: the nurse, the doctor, the medication, and the lifestyle choices. I had to keep trying all of it because no one person or thing gave me the full answer I needed.

I am telling you now what you have to do. You have to take responsibility for your life, your bipolar, and you need to learn what you need in every minute of the day. You are responsible for your thoughts, actions, and emotions. Later we can relax more when we achieve a tendency for balance and health through thought, action, and feeling habits. We can cruise on auto-pilot and many of the little things will take care of themselves. We are new persons with strong lives, yet in my experience bipolar raises its head once in a while to see if it can come out and rule my life again.

We have the tools of medications and doctors to assist us. Never before in our history have we bipolar people had the powers to counter the negatives of this illness and tap into the gift. It starts in your thoughts. Can you beat this thing? You have much to think and do and feel. You can learn to feel great in spite of the circumstances—not that you will ignore what is going on around you, but you have the power to choose joy and possibility.

You can compose your loops of thought and develop new regions of joy and peace in your life and brain. Think big and dream—feel your dream and step toward it now. Learn from your mistakes in thinking and struggle to know the many ways that can influence your thinking, actions, and emotions.

With bipolar you can control your moods and extremes. You will be released from your treadmill ruts. You can learn to live at the equator of your mood. You will have kept the extremes within you to harness and use their energy and mindset and you will eventually arrive at an easier place of life. Things will flow and you won't have to work as hard, but you will make bigger advances because of all your past effort.

You will swim in the warm Caribbean waters and feel the fresh breeze. Enjoy the juice. You will have earned it. Feel the triumph. I heard somewhere that triumph is umph added to try. We will try and try through it all. We will fall down and lose our sanity and may visit suicidal thinking again, but we will learn quicker ways to balance our lives. Enjoy. The struggle will get easier.

Points of thought and action:

#1   What recordings do I play?

#2   Who or what triggers my loops of thought?

#3   Which loops are positive and which are negative?

#4   What recordings do I need to create and memorize to grow the positive?

#5   What new prompt balance cards do I need to create and use?

#6   (My personal plan.)

MUSIC

Is there power, peace, and motivation in music? We are all affected differently by noise and sound. What is horrible noise to one ear is sweet music to another. How does music affect us? Do you need to make your own? I need to at times. Does certain music help you to sleep? I listen to white noise at times, static FM, and it helps me let go to sleep; at other times I find it irritating.

I like the sounds of nature, waterfalls and pounding surf. Moving water in general is a good base for my peace. City sounds of progress generally stress me out. Loud mufflers on vehicles make me hike my shoulders. Maybe I am getting old but I like peace and quiet. I love to hear laughter and children at play: I don't like to hear them whine or scream. To my ears we shouldn't need to honk horns to lock our cars with our convenient little gadgets. Is this kind to our souls? It is not beneficial to mine. I hate the beeps in fast food restaurants and the electronic noises in our world—they usually put me on edge, but I am learning to adapt and tune out.

I appreciate many forms and styles of music. I heard a classical piece on the radio last night that touched my soul in ways I did not know I needed. As part of our leaving our illness we need to experiment with music to discover comfort and to commune with the wilderness of our soul. Perhaps you have real sad music that you bring out when you are feeling down and out—it helps you to not feel alone. You cry and hit your bottom and rise up, you put on different music that lifts you further—you are on your way. You can build your music collection like a toolkit to effect your moods toward what you need.

On occasion, I love the mix of heavy metal and classical. *Metallica's S & M* project with the San Francisco Symphony moves me to a better place. It enhances me to be a better person. I can't listen to it all the time. But when I do, it carries me to a brighter world, it soothes and rocks me and carries me and throws me to the winds. It balances and propels me. The extremes talk to me and renew my gift. It reacquaints me with the best parts of bipolar: the sensuality, the energy, the intensity, the sexuality, the depth, the paradox, the beauty, the enhancement, the force, and the flow.

What do you like? You may not like any music at all and silence is your forte. I believe silence is the backdrop to all, all that is here—as we reduce silence, everything else is distorted and we need to find replacements for our soul's need for quiet. I believe this one point is a huge contributor to our modern problems—clutter of things and noise can cause a tendency for a cluttered mind. A mind that is muddled and self-sabotaging doesn't even know who it is, and more noise and things are thrown in for good measure. Then we forever shift our activity and place searching for solution; but the solution waits within us, to slow down and embrace our internal stillness and who we are.

Certain minor musical keys have the ability to immediately connect to us in an emotional way. We can use this in a positive manner to help us feel something when we need to in our cool emotional states. And it can help us to be aware of why we are more emotional when we are listening to certain music, or even an advertising jingle. Certain cultures have unique musical emotional triggers. China has different musical keys to affect people than the western world. There is even a chord named the devil's chord that was banned back in church history. It is used in heavy metal music. Perhaps that is why I like on occasion the mix of metal and classical. The contrast and extremes speaks to my bipolar experience.

Like our hard drives, we need to de-fragment our mind. We need silence but rarely get it. It is where we can think and revel in our reflections and ponderings; it is where we fear our thoughts and wanderings and leanings. Perhaps we all need to face down our silence—our existence of self speaks loud in times of inactivity. Have you ever tried to brave your hinterlands? It may be one of your keys away from illness. Silence can frighten yet illuminate your needs. Practice turning off electronics and learn to listen to the silence and you will develop wisdom and all you need to live greatly. Meditation will help with your processing. Study and practice meditation—there are many forms. It will be a template of peace that you can insert into your mind in times of turmoil.

There is power in music to help us with our inlets, processing, and outlets. On occasion, classical music is a balm to my over-fired synapses: my overworked processing brain finds classical strings to be a soothing balm. You can play an instrument, bang a drum or hit a pen against a surface. It might make you feel better: it is a physical release. Some exercise consists of a secondary music making—you beat out a rhythm with your body or feet and perhaps this is part of why we feel better. I was in the army cadets for a year and the marching has revisited me on occasion—it has helped in discipline and the simple left, right, left, right has given me a focus on certain tough psychotic marches. And perhaps the training conditioned me to go there in my psychosis.

Make music and celebrate your life. Try something new. We can all contribute musically in some way. A simple flute or drum will help us emotionally as a great outlet. I find that my guitar playing bores me at times: it can be uninspired, but at other times it is inspired and beautiful and carries me to another place and brings me back a better person.

We as bipolar people can have advantages in following our muse, our inner guide to creativity. In living with madness we traveled to other places and times and moods: therefore we can be entwined to creative leanings in a tighter manner. We can listen to guidance and trust that we will journey and be okay. My writing blows me away at times when I let go and trust the calling. The muse can speak quickly and with effect.

I heard a great blues musician interviewed and he talked candidly about his bipolar—he had in the past self-medicated with booze and drugs and lived a challenging existence. The interviewer suggested that his playing was much deeper and full of emotion for being bipolar. The guitarist agreed that it made him a better player. They played a couple of his tunes and indeed the depth and fullness of his playing shone above the norm. You could feel his notes resonate with nuances of feeling and expression.

Bipolar can be used to become a better musician. You can be a better listener. I am more open to a wide range of emotion in music and I am aware of how music can help change my mood. It is one of the tools I use to tweak my mood and headspace.

Be careful with it. I was a little bit up years ago and getting ready for some in-line skating. I listened to *Soundgarden* to get ready and then I listened to *Kiss Unplugged* to skate. The music gave me more courage and disrespect for my safety. It surged my feeling of hypo and made me lose touch with my speed and place. I had to choose between an intersection and grass; I did not have brakes and did not want to slide the skate sideways. I chose the grass and attempted a front tuck and roll—not enough tuck and my shoulder grabbed and separated. The music was a contributing factor.

Music holds power to heal and to motivate. Make your mental and paper notes of how you are affected by each piece of music. Use it as part of your toolkit. You can reduce your illness and increase your balance and gift with music. It is yours to utilize. Each piece of music in your collection will act like a recipe on your mood to help strike your balance.

Enjoy making music with your life. Let your songs out.

Points of thought and action:

#1　How does each type of my music affect me?

#2　What sounds and music are good for me and how?

#3　What sounds and music are bad for me and how?

#4　Do I have music inside me that needs to get out?

#5　How can I embrace and learn from silence?

#6　(My personal plan.)

EXERCISE

We as a society are only beginning to experience the ill effects of our sedate lifestyles. It will get worse. What is your need for exercise? When do you need it most? How does the lack of exercise affect you? I get bitchy, impatient, and don't sleep well. I don't think as well, I'm not happy or as optimistic. I get a sore body with symptoms similar to fibromyalgia. My muscles ache. My joints hurt. The last thing I want to do is exercise. I hate it.

When I became depressed, exercise was the last thing I was capable of; and I don't mean the type of depression that is thrown around lightly. It bothers me that people speak so quickly of their depression. I see someone dressed and functioning and talking and smiling—someone who has no right to speak of depression. Go and sit with a catatonic depressive for an hour and tell me about feeling blue. Certainly there are many layers of depression, but do you agree that the term is overused?

Our bodies are designed to move. Look at every other living mammal—they move. If they don't move it can usually be traced to human interference—an example could be a dog that is overfed the wrong food. If you do not move enough and in ways that are suitable for your body type, you will suffer consequences. If you do not use it, you will lose it.

I am no elite athlete and do not want to spend the time to become one. I like to be able to physically perform certain tasks. I like to hike up to a waterfall, paddle a canoe, and go for a walk. I am over forty and am happy with my condition. I have been heavier and lighter. I have been skinny to the point of ill-health: I was weak and cold and had little muscle. I have had more fat on my body and felt terrible. Medication packed on the pounds. Our medications and illness can change our bodies in a real hurry. We can wake up to being bipolar and have gained a hundred pounds in the process. It is not the end: it is a journey. You can make it wherever you want to go a step at a time.

I love the fact that muscle burns more calories than fat, even at rest. I can sleep and burn those chips and chocolates off quicker if I have more muscle. When I can, I try to build muscle mass and keep moving. I try to walk a lot. It is a struggle—our places of progress make it more dangerous and uncomfortable to be a pedestrian. We are engineered to drive to the stores and shop. Try to walk between box store developments and see how low a priority walking is. Look both ways before you cross the street. I no longer like to walk with my back to the on-coming traffic.

With bipolar I find exercise is a cornerstone to good health. It helps me deal with hypo energy and it brings me back to balance. The resulting endorphins are great medicine. It has been one of my routes out of depression. When I went down, I would sleep for three quarters of the day. I did not want to exercise. My back would get sore from staying in bed. My whole body was a mess. I played loud fast music to get me out the door. I wore headphones to propel me. I walked. I swam. I in-line skated. We do what little we can and celebrate the achievement.

I found by approaching exercise while manic or heading high, I had to be careful. All this crazy energy and my body was limited. There were points where I crossed over and injured myself. It can be great to channel your high energy into exercise, but there is a point where it is too much energy and you need to start controlling it through other means, including medication.

When I was manic I could suddenly run a marathon, but my body would give out on me. Our bodies send messages. We need to rest. We need to know ourselves. Medication and bipolar can block the pain messages. Treading water in a pool with a lifeguard present would be safer and tend to be injury-free compared to running.

Mania and medication and depression can cause you to be out of touch with your body. Be careful to not overdue it and cause injury. I once ran manic and hurt my foot: it was terrible to be hampered in movement. All this energy and I limped. Then a doctor gave me an anti-inflammatory and this seemed to cross with my tranquilizers to make me paranoid. It didn't help that I was in Cuba at the time. Things can snowball on us and we need to counter the small things before they grow and attract other problems.

Sometimes in depression I had slipped into doing nothing for weeks: it was a slow climb out. It was a feat to just get dressed and put shoes on. If you are stuck with no movement, get dressed and put shoes on and step outside, take a breath and turn around and go back inside. If you can't get dressed, try to brush your teeth, anything you are able to do is great. Celebrate your achievement. You are amazing. Reward yourself. Do something else. Tomorrow you can do a little more. Pamper your body and thoughts.

You are different. You need to do certain things. Be nice to yourself. Start out slow—talk to your doctor. That sounded funny. Use it or lose it. There is great information available on exercise. Just move and listen to your body for what it needs to develop and rest. Feed yourself well. How do you like to move your body? Dancing, sex, cleaning your house, and playing with a child are all great activities. Do things that are fun and it will be easier to find motivation.

Exercise helps the body achieve and maintain balance. We are designed to move. It helps sleep and appetite and sex. It helps us to reduce illness and our need for medication. It can help keep us out of the hospital. It can help us touch and live the gift that is bipolar.

Points of thought and action:
#1   What happens to me when I don't exercise?
#2   How does exercise affect my mood, thoughts, stress level, and sleep?
#3   How do I place precautions to not hurt my body when I am energized or out of touch?
#4   How do I like to move and what can I do right now?
#5   How can I motivate myself to exercise?
#6   (My personal plan.)

FOOD

Are we truly what we eat? I love to eat—sometimes I don't care if it is good for me or not. I want it to taste good. Bring on the fat and the sugar. Sooner or later we pay the price. I loved to eat butter and eggs—I developed high cholesterol. The doctor wanted to put me on medication for it. I asked for a chance to change it on my own. I exercised more and researched the latest food choices to change it. I eliminated the butter and eggs and ate more almonds, soya, rice bran, and oat bran with oatmeal. These few changes turned it around.

When I saw my doctor and he saw my new lab results, he was surprised. He thought he had put me on medication.

I said, "No I did it with diet."

"What did you do?" the doctor asked me and then closed his ears.

He has been trained to approach problems from one major angle—medication. I have a new doctor who is wise in many approaches.

By how many angles do you approach your bipolar? You have approaches of health that I have never thought of. We have to consider the food we eat.

Certain foods slightly affect our dopamine and serotonin levels. Do you crave types of foods at specific times of the year? Before a cold snap do you crave heavier foods? Do you eat lighter in hot weather? How do your moods affect your appetite? Does any food help you in your moods? Food is a personal thing and your body needs different food than mine does. There are similarities though—servings of fruits and vegetables can help prevent bowel cancer and other problems in all of us.

Sugar can take me on a good ride: I fly up and then I crash. If sugar was all I ate, I would be a mess. Complex sugars are better for you—the ones found in fruits and other foods.

I struggled with enough, just to be able to eat, back in my poverty days. And depending on my condition, I was not able to prepare much food. I found it to be a great assistance in bipolar to be able to eat on a regular basis. To this day I still eat smaller amounts and more often. When I get hungry I tend to get bitchy and impatient. And it can go from there—my head grows in the negative focus. If my stomach has something to focus on, my head tends to be on straight.

In my times of hypo and running the risk of entering full blown mania, one thing I would do is eat a good hearty meal. If I was out, a basic burger and fries with gravy did the trick. It filled me up and slowed me down a bit—my blood would rush to my gut to deal with the food and I would want to sit or lay down. I would be on medication for mania too. An hour later I might have been flying high once again, but you need to wear a problem down with as many solutions as possible. That hour of rest was good for me—it gave my system a chance to renew. There is the point of running on adrenaline and mania alone. You feed on your own flesh eventually—you break down. Food can be a way of pacing. And please—don't just eat burgers, fries, and gravy.

I try to eat a healthy balance. I tend to do better with natural unprocessed foods—they make me feel better and provide optimum fuel. In my depression, I ate less but I still ate. It was one thing I got out of bed for. I tried to eat simple foods because I was not that active. But I also pampered myself by eating comfort foods. What food makes you feel warm and comfy?

In mixed states it makes sense to stay away from sugar and quick processed foods. Grab onto any anchor you can—a meal that slows you down may help in your mood bouncing around. When I went high, food seemed to rush through me. I would feel thin and hollow, I bounced with energy and movement and thoughts that raced. Meat was one thing that took a little longer to digest and it seemed to assist me. I have counted as many as fifty to sixty bowel movements per day when I was manic. I believe it had something to do with the smooth muscle action of the bowels—it is an involuntary, nervous aspect. Irritable bowel syndrome is similar. I would eat something and it would go right through me. My digestion seemed to be sped right up. It helped to eat bigger meals but I was so far gone that the main thing I could do was medication to counter the mania.

One thing I have done several times is a cleanse of my digestive system. I bought a package of supplements from the health food store; included is a balanced cheap diet with many vegetables. They break the foods into categories of alkaline and neutral and acidic. You are allowed a certain proportion from each category. This is how I woke up to the fact that I should only drink a maximum of two cups of coffee a day. Have you seen how large the heartburn, acid reflux section is in large stores? How many products do we need to save us? Find out what foods are acidic and cut down on a few of them and you will be released from your dependence on these products. If you have problems with heartburn, your body is telling you something about your diet. Eat more alkaline and less acidic: more vegetables and fruit and less coffee, sugar, and white flour.

After the cleanse, and eating non-processed foods and no sugar for ten days your system works incredibly well. Your body takes in the nutrients efficiently and you work from a clean slate. We tend to take on some new food items from the suggested foods. There are a lot of great vegetables in the world.

I seem to go through phases of good and bad. I am open genetically to diabetes and I need to keep my weight down and exercise and eat healthy. Perhaps an adult provided a certain food with their love for you when you were growing up. We can't use it as an excuse—we have to be aware of our learned patterns and gain control.

I buy healthy snacks and have caches in the car and in the cupboards. I reach and eat something before I am caving in from hunger—even if the snacks are only a little healthy, it is better than capitulating and super-sizing.

Chocolate can be a habit for me—we started having dark chocolate around with sugar not being the first ingredient. It took me a while to get used to the 70 to 85% cocoa content. I like it now. I found that I am less dependent on it—what I thought was a slight chocolate dependency was actually the sugar. If I eat sugary chocolate for a few days in a row I tend to want it everyday. Chocolate can give me a little emotional warmth and soothing—this has been supported with studies that relate it to being in love.

As bipolar people we need to watch the stimulants. Being on too much medication such as a tranquilizer sets us up to need stimulants to function. Coffee can be hard on your adrenal gland and digestive system. Using sugar and caffeine can be symptoms of our mood and medication. Try to recognize the patterns in the foods you crave—what does it mean? Add it to your chart. What are your habits with food? I remember having coffee with a fellow manic years ago and he put a third of a cup of sugar in his coffee cup. It overflowed and made me laugh but it reminds me of the hypo stage—sometimes I self-medicated with sugar and caffeine and chocolate to keep revved up. These alone can be dangerous for some of us. Binge before bed on this trinity and you may not sleep before sunrise—it could be your occasional form of self-sabotage.

When I work my muscles hard, I crave protein—my body wants to rebuild. I find with the onset of fall and winter I want heavier foods and more pasta. I tend to reward myself with small treats and spread them out. I just ate an apple and in a while I will treat myself with a candy. How does your diet affect you? If you want to be awake and alive to enjoy your gift you do not want heart disease, diabetes or obesity getting in your way.

It is horrible that weight gain can be part of our medication treatment. Sometimes a doctor can over-medicate to make us easier to manage: we are less threatening as potential manics if we are covered in drug. A side concern of not being able to move much is you lose muscle tissue and then you burn fewer calories. We have to deal with it to get to a balance. We have to exercise and eat in moderation. And like certain street drugs, medications can give us a case of the munchies. I remember getting the growlies from certain tranquilizers: pass the mayonnaise and butter, pass the gravy—let me savor the fat now. Certain medications have dietary restrictions: talk to your pharmacist about your medication precautions.

Eating disorders are horrible beasts to deal with. Bipolar can take us to their fringes and open the door. Those are tough places to return from. It is similar to our challenge with taking addictive medications if we have addiction issues—we need drugs at times to survive. Eating disorder people need food to survive. Total abstinence is not possible. I have absolute respect for people who surmount their eating issues and live in balance.

A certain way for me to approach a hypo productive state is to work physically for a period of time without eating. I can be working on the house, cleaning or whatever, and I am starting to get hungry and don't eat and continue moving, I get spun out and get more physical and can get a lot done. It isn't true hypo; it is more like sheer movement that gets less and less thought involved. I stop moving and eat and come back to my senses. I try to not go there often, it doesn't feel healthy and it can be dangerous, I fell on some stairs once in this condition. Food is my remedy in such states.

Ideally with bipolar shifts in mood and activity levels, we should adjust our diets accordingly. In times of lethargy and inactivity with depression, we should eat fewer calories. This would be tough if you have the depressive tendency of eating more. I was lucky and tended to eat less, mostly because I lacked any initiative—I'd rather sleep than get food. We need to eat at least small amounts to keep our systems working. If we skip breakfast we can trick our bodies into storing extra fat, our bodies are complex and have amazing survival mechanisms.

Talk to a nutritionist. It can be a challenge when we are not in our right mind. I have been admitted to hospital and stood in front of the food machines with a few dollars and thought I was in the afterlife. The fanciest packaging grabbed my attention—it did not matter what it was. I loved those wild color schemes when I was manic. And why have hospitals taken so long to remove the junk food in their snack machines? Is everything about profit with no responsibility for the future? Without sick people we would not need hospitals. Do we really have power to improve our health? I believe we do, in more ways than you can count. Your diet is one leg to stand on. You are what you consume. Be easy on yourself. It takes time. Forgive your binges and move on.

I find cooking is a release and passion. I get keyed up with life and I can mellow and enjoy the creative pursuit of cooking. I love to combine new ingredients into new results. I love to eat and cook. It is part of my gift.

Hey, I still haven't eaten that candy—that apple went a long way. Bipolar forces us to be aware of details in our lives. You can run and hide but that approach keeps you in the negative of this opportunity. We need to face our diets and take responsibility to know how what we consume affects our mood and life.

You are able to educate yourself and be empowered to better your quality of life with your food and drink. You can get lots of information on food and how it affects you. Check out your library. You can live long and strong in your gift. This illness can make us brilliant racecars that require optimum fuel for our performance.

Points of thought and action:

#1   What food and drink items affect my mood?

#2   Does my medication trigger cravings for food?

#3   How can I eat differently to help my present situation of mania or depression?

#4   Do I have any eating disorder concerns wrapped up in my behavior?

#5   What is a change I can make in my lifestyle to gain or lose weight?

#6   (My personal plan.)

SUPPLEMENTS

In parts of Europe, St. John's Wort is used more for depression than anti-depressants are. And in North America we are putting our children, even our infants on anti-depressants. Hello? Do infants need to be on major drugs that can cause side effects in their formative years? Perhaps these children, like our dying fish in our rivers and oceans, are warning signs.

Supplements can have power for us. Be careful—it is tough to wade through the topic. But it can be worthwhile and beneficial. The pharmaceutical system was totally against the use of natural supplements until they learned how much money could be made. In my area of residence no drugstore exists that does not focus on health food supplements.

If your diet is not exceptional you need to take multivitamins—we cannot live in balance in the gift eating the same item, or not a good variety. You may want to talk to your nutritionist and doctor and pharmacist and health food person about taking supplements. I like to talk to a health food store employee who knows their products. You do need to be careful about what you take and how much—it may interfere with your medications and treatment plan. Talk to your doctor. I like doctors who are open minded to the subject of diet and supplements. I wonder about a doctor's brain if he or she only thinks about pharmaceuticals and bashes diet and supplements.

We have very few studies performed on these natural products; therefore the hype is either they are dangerous or unproven to do anything, or they are better than they are. Some are dangerous. We also have the placebo effect that can be powerful. You could take a simple pill that does nothing physically but you believe that it will work and it does work. Wow—belief is a beautiful thing.

Try to work with your doctor and build trust with a health food practitioner. For this inner ear problem that I have, my wife talked to a lady in the health food part of a pharmacy and she gave more guidance than my medical doctor did. It's a weird world. She gave us direction to a better exercise and awareness of the problem.

Do your research and due diligence. Check out orthomolecular—it can perform wonders with certain people. Megavitamin treatments have been used with great effect with mental illness. I like to use a homeopathic product named Calms and Rescue Remedy—they help me mellow out and I like that there are no side effects. It is our responsibility to get well and stay well. Medications can work on serotonin and dopamine levels which are connected to mood: food and supplements can also affect serotonin and dopamine. These levels can be connected to our food cravings and even the time of year cravings. Winter can bring on certain cravings. There are supplements that can assist in balancing our dopamine and serotonin levels. Talk to your experts.

They can be confusing and expensive. Yet supplements can be used to minimize your use of medications. This is a great thing because we all hear the announcements about certain medications, that are now causing heart attacks or other complications, being pulled off the shelf. Supplements are one angle of approach to life that can reduce our extremes and help us live in balance and the gift, perhaps with a little less medication. Talk to your doctor.

I am working in a place where my diet is inadequate. I am taking greens, a natural way to get more of the nutrients I need. It may be the best thing I can do for myself in this increased stress environment. If we do not eat properly we will get ill. We need to eat well or take supplements and preferably both. Be careful and use them like any other thing. They can help save or hinder your life—we need to be wise to the possible effects and use them responsibly.

Cost can be a factor—there are simple solutions. A three-dollar carton of blackstrap molasses is full of B vitamins—good for the brain. Perhaps take a spoonful a day. Oat and rice bran and Soya help with cholesterol. Apples and carrots are good roughage. All of these and more are available for less cost than a fast food meal. Chamomile tea could be listed as a supplement. It is not expensive and could help you with your sleep. Peppermint tea is good for an upset stomach.

A friend of mine did a lot of research on the field of supplements and came up with the motto "rotation and moderation." Too much of anything can be a bad thing and you need to give things a rest and do something else. We are still connected to the seasons and nature and we need to be aware of how this affects our diet.

Enjoy your supplements and make them work for you. It takes time and don't worry, it is best at times to not even go there—you have plenty to think about. It is the same with any subject—if it is stressing you out let it go and concentrate on what helps you feel good and in balance.

Good orderly direction will help you on your road. Maybe you need to take the full drug regimen for a few months and get stable and then you can introduce a certain supplement. Do your homework and take it easy. You'll get there in time. Look on the bright side and live well in this day. Feel good about where you are and you will tend to feel better about your tomorrow.

Supplements are there to help you in reaching your gift.

Points of thought and action:

#1   Is my diet varied and healthy?

#2   Should I take supplements?

#3   Are there more economical solutions to my dietary and supplement needs?

#4   What are some supplements that I need to stay away from on my medication? (Pharmacist.)

#5   How does what I take help me?

#6   (My personal plan.)

WACKY WAYS TO HEALTH

Anything can help us to heal and live in balance. And something is wacky only because of the filter you look through. Talk to enough people about any approach and you will eventually be judged as wacky, this includes the approach of traditional doctors and medication. We need to be aware of our needs and be open.

Acupuncture, homeopathy, orthomolecular, pets, visiting old people, massage, and reflexology. Whatever helps you out is great. The simple touch of another is amazing. Performing acts of kindness has power. We all need unique experiences to help us heal. Maybe you want to try hypnotherapy, maybe it freaks you out. Maybe you like to pray in a group. Anything is great if you use it for good.

I believe intent is powerful in determining whether something is evil or good. The internet can be used for child porn—or medical advice and healing. Any form or approach to healing can be the same—it is the intent of your heart. Certain religious pursuits can judge other angles of passion. And non-spiritual people judge spiritual people. We can get caught up in all the judging and comparing and not be healed or live well. We need to have more love and peace and joy in our lives. I don't think many people would argue with that.

When we are open to healing, we need to trust its many forms and not judge. Cuba has a place in my heart because the people accepted me in my state of mania and this acceptance was part of my healing. Perhaps that breakthrough could not have occurred elsewhere.

Find out what heals you and use it for your good. Learn what does not harm you or others and use it for your benefit. Do your research and trials. Some of the best things in life are free. A baby will smile back at you and shine light into your soul. Where have they been to do this? Why does the world wear this down? Part of my living well is to get babies to smile. Wouldn't it be great if we all worked this way? Smiles are contagious and take fewer muscles.

There are as many ways to find healing as numbers of people. We all have unique approaches. Is it not bizarre that I needed to watch horror movies to get over my psychotic episodes? Growing fruit helps me to live well; what is produced from the ground astounds me. Listen to your heart and mind and you will get in touch with your intuition. You will feel the detail in you and follow it to conclusion. Sometimes it is trial and error. Practice and you will get there. Go for a walk and use your intuition to turn left or right. Maybe it will take you to a special position, a place of trees and light that soothes your soul.

It is a wonderful world of healing out there. You will have your own safe harbors that are yours alone. Give me a warm bath and a candle and some cello music and it will sand down my troubled feeling. There are times I have no clue why something is occurring and that is the time I need to simply accept and move to a kinder place. I can suddenly feel down and out and I need to move toward fetal position in a closet for a time. I have done this and listened to the urge, it felt best to have clothes strewn about me. I cannot explain it but I did it and it helped—I have not had the urge in a long time and maybe because I listened to it, I no longer have the need.

When I was manic and psychotic in the hospital I liked to shower fully clothed. I do not know why—maybe I was dry and needed the water to hydrate and cool. But I remember my doctor being amused by it, and it sounded like I was not the only one. Why do we do these things? I think to get back to a balance and health. They can be tricky pursuits that require solitude and care, and support. Not everyone can give you this support.

I remember taking a friend out into nature after a long winter in the city. The snow was melting and there was a stream flowing. I left him alone and he was drawn to the flowing water and he anointed himself and bathed in the fresh water. He was a man of insane visitations and perhaps an attachment to nature was missing from his life: the city coldness was part of his problem. He was a happy free man after his spring cleansing.

Chopping wood and simple cleaning can take stress away. Cleaning windows or vacuuming could be your secret to help get through your tough times. Rearrange your furniture. You are unique and special. Bake a cake or build a birdhouse. Make something useful out of broken or junk items. Give away some of your clothes you never wear. Organize your closets and pass on items that you never use—make room for the things you do need. The list of potential acts is endless.

And there are many organized healing methods that cost money. I am seeing a homeopath and taking remedies and I swear that it is enhancing my life and its gift. A few years ago I was not open to this and now it feels like an icing-on-the-cake type of experience. There are many free modes of healing. Practicing prayer or meditation are wonderful modes of healing. Walk in nature. I believe that the bipolar gift is to discover who you really are—an enhanced self-realized human.

Bipolar can stretch us to be more of an introvert and extrovert and to have more interests. You will live in balance and in time you will help other people—it is part of living in balance. Live the gift.

Points of thought and action:
#1   What is an unusual thing that I've done that helped me?
#2   How did it help me and why?
#3   What is something I felt the urge to do and thought it might help, but didn't do?
#4   What is something I need to try today?
#5   Does it matter what others may think, if it helps me and ultimately helps them out?
#6   (My personal plan.)

DISCIPLINE

We need the order and balance of discipline in our lives as bipolar people. We must struggle to the place of self-discipline. It can take years but it is a major aspect of leaving the illness. We have to be tough on ourselves, we have to be kind and know when to push and change.

Sometimes bipolar is our chemistry driving our thinking, actions, and emotions: we need to talk to our doctor and use our medication. We can also look sometimes at bipolar as the lack of discipline in the mind, we are carried by the whims of how we feel and think—we are controlled. We have to consciously decide to take back responsibility for our moods, and discipline is our structure for doing so. Self-awareness opens approaches to remedy, and discipline creates consistent and motivated action to achieve changes in our mood and life.

If you want to increase your discipline, study and practice it. Perhaps you need to borrow someone else's discipline—is there a martial art or sport or dance that you could take? The mental discipline to move toward mastery in these physical arts will spill into other areas of your life. An instructor or sensei will hold you accountable to what you have chosen to study. Does someone in your support network play the role of lifestyle coach for you? Grant people you trust power over you to ensure that you live your empowered choices.

It takes incredible self-control to live in a psychiatric center. The place can drive you wild—people scream and cry and talk nonsense, and pace. The condition that sent us in is challenging enough. If you are a person who is sensitive to others it can be an over-stimulating place. You have to develop discipline to walk away to a quieter place, to your room. You have to make choices to guard your sanity; headphones can be a form of self-protection.

You have to unwind toward sleep. It takes practice to embrace a bedtime routine—it is discipline to not choose too stimulating events or substances. You have to take the pill and quiet your mind: sometimes we can consciously slow our thoughts, but when there is sheer chemical-vibrated thinking, medication is most effective. At other times, audio of ocean waves and nice music or relaxation exercises will assist you.

Each time that I went manic, I would start smoking. I would quit in my depression and in good months. Then I would start again. It was a cycle that culminated in year round smoking for a couple of years. There were times that it seemed medicinal for me but overall it was bad. I kept trying and finally broke the habit. It helped me to write out my triggers—where and when I would light up. It also helped to write down the reasons I wanted to quit. The last time I quit, I used the nicotine patch for a few weeks, and chewed on straws and gum... anything that helps you is good.

If you have performed any of the exercises in this book you have good self-discipline. You are on your way to a better life. If some of the techniques, such as the hope chest, or prompt to-do lists when you are high or low or mixed, are new to you, they may make you feel empowered, which is great. Celebrate your achievement of performing these tasks and do something nice as a reward.

Think about using these techniques for your balance to avoid the extremes. Do you anticipate any pitfalls or problems? It can be great on paper but when we apply it to our lives it can get messy. Very often repeated failure must be embraced and fought through with discipline before any breakthrough. Toward the last couple of years of my major mess of bipolar, I had the sensation of being in a tunnel; I could feel in my bones that I was to be spit out of the struggle and strife, that I would be released soon. I kept working on what made me better in balance and it happened—I had the sensation of being launched out of the dark pipe. Years of hard work and discipline and suffering finally paid off. I was out of the pipe.

To get better with bipolar we have to be rebels of discipline with self-knowledge. Our society generally wants us to consume TV and radio and consumer goods. Advertisers tell us how to think. We don't even have to think, others will do it for us. The medical system tends to still be others caring for us. What they say is best for us. And that is great, because most of us have not got the foggiest idea of what we need, nor do we have the discipline to perform those new thoughts and actions.

Will you strive to be different? Will you learn to know what you need at any given minute, to know how everything you choose, and the things that just happen, affect you? Do you treat your health and mind like a fortress? Are you careful what you put into it? Do you make it stronger with, or choose to numb it with, TV? Listen to old radio plays and it will strengthen your mind through providing images. You have to make the video up in your head and these strengths of images will spin into other areas of your life—your thinking will be tighter and you will have stronger links to depend on in times of need.

Perhaps if we strengthened our discipline of mind, psychosis and depression and mixed states would have less power to maim and kill. Learn something new to develop your brain—this will spill positively into your discipline to deal with the negative of bipolar. Anything I do that increases my mental energy and activity and endurance will have effect in times of assault from the crazies. You have all this solid material in your head that you can depend on in attack. To recite poems can be a refuge from mistaken and rapid thinking. You are your mind and what you think of.

Let's use our minds to ponder this subject: do you think that if you develop mental energy, activity, and endurance; it will be an advantage in your times of attack with the crazies? There is a point where having the wherewithal and discipline to remember and to take your medication will save you from extremes. What about remembering your children, who need you, at certain times of suicidal thinking. Maybe you think that only medication will help those physiological chemical swirls of brain. What about the beginning slices of craze?

Those hours and days where our sleep could go either way, if we are numb patients waiting for our next appointment to have our doctor guide us through this illness, and we do nothing but our medication and things that make us worse or just things that are indifferent. If we don't exercise, we only drink coffee and take our anxiety medication; will anything make a difference? Will living your life with few regrets make a difference? What about treating people horribly? What about never having dealt with the father that beat you as a child?

You will come up with different angles than me on this subject. I hope that the heavens have opened up and you see the light that any and every thing can affect and cause effect on our moods of bipolar. You are in control of your life even with a major mental illness called bipolar disorder. If you use it as an excuse, it will make your whole life an excuse. If you explain your horrible actions always with the illness cause, this madness thing will continue to drag you down its powerful rails toward harm and destruction.

Will you lay on the ground in the fetal position with this predator chewing on you? Or are you going to fight back? Show the mad monster that you are the top bear around your parts—bipolar you'd better back down. Are you going to study to be a monk athlete in your lifestyle? You can prevent much suffering in your future.

Cutting down on your caffeine and sugar, improving your diet, exercising, and studying and practicing relaxation and sleep hygiene will lessen your need for tranquilizers. Reduced tranquilizers mean fewer side effects. Being a monk athlete in these areas alone may prevent you from getting Tardive Dyskinesia. And if you have it already that is all right, you can still make changes to improve your life. Take control with discipline to make the small soldiers of change rise up into an army to counter the attacks of craze. Install systems of good thought and action that are a framework of discipline to hold your positive middle ground.

It takes discipline to avoid the hospital, to take medication when it makes you feel horrible, but works. It is tough to not commit suicide, to call the crisis line instead. We need to be tough to deal with bipolar. If you are not tough now, you will get tougher, and you will either get bitter and unhappy, or you will choose to be happy and joyous and move your life onward and upward.

And you will choose and develop your new life of possibility in hope and renewal. You can change your habits and transform into your designed way of life. You can create your own existence and know that you are living the gift; your life the way you need to live it.

Points of thought and action:
#1   What self-discipline comes easily to me?
#2   How can I use this ease to strengthen other areas of my life?
#3   What self-discipline am I currently helpless at?

#4 Can I increase my reward anticipation to get it done and then treat myself?

#5 What do I need to do right now to improve my mood and balance?

#6 (My personal plan.)

WEATHER OR NOT ENVIRONMENT

Here I come on a Chinook wind. Look out, I'm flying. A Chinook wind passes over the Rocky Mountains and compresses and ionizes. Around the world, there are the Mistral, the Shiraz, and the Santa Ana: similar winds with the same effect. Back in history, crimes of murder committed under the effects of this wind have been pardoned. Does the weather affect us? Or were those superstitious times?

I believe that back in history we were more in touch with our bodies, environments, and the weather—we had to know and respond to survive. We are far removed from nature now. Does the weather still have any effect on you? I grew up on the prairie where the sun was strong and the winter cold. We had one of the highest levels of sunshine in our country and people smiled and were friendly. As an adult I moved toward the foothills of the Rockies where the Chinook blew. Winter seemed too long and then the Chinook thawed and sent me high and manic. I allowed it to ride me.

In retrospect I believe that I was not living my life in balance as I should have been and the warming just provided the final nudge. We can be precarious creatures affected by the smallest of externals. Our internal power of processing and changing the language of our self-talk can be weak at times; and the weather can conspire with other forces at those times to have more affect.

Science is out studying weather phenomenon and how it affects us. Seattle, Washington is a center for seasonal affective disorder research— they have dark wet winters. I now live on the same coast and can attest to the effects of this dark season. In the last six weeks we have had one sunny day that represented approximately seventy five percent of the day. We have had a couple of twenty percent sunny days. In total, in the last six weeks, we have had full-blown sunshine for maybe twelve hours.

I used light therapy this last rainy season and it helped me with the blues. Do your research; perhaps some light therapy would assist you. Be careful to not overdo it. Remember it is small things that add up and merge to win the war. Light therapy for some people is revolutionary in helping them.

Maybe this is one of the reasons that tanning beds do such good business—it is a form of self-medicating to relax and feel good. These are trade offs from the darkened skin and health risks.

I have a hard time adjusting to a lack of sunshine, it brings me down and I think and feel gloomy. If I do not exercise I will slide—I can feel it. It is tough to be motivated and outgoing. People are more reserved and inside more: we talk with and see our neighbors less. It is raining and the plus side is that we have green and no snow to scrape and shovel. We had the Pineapple Express weather from Hawaii the other week and it brought people up, making them more happy and extroverted. It was a warm trend that felt great. I felt up and happier: there was no more sunshine, but warmth to the air. People were out and about smiling and talking more.

How does the weather affect you? When we have full-blown sunshine out of this dark it will feel wonderful. I will be working in a winter climate in a couple of weeks where it is cold but sunny. I will absorb it to my core and feel calmer and happier. Our wet season depends on the year. Last year did not have this long of stretch without sun. I feel like this is a great place to live but my ideal is to live in a sunny climate through this dark gloom. I can live here but it is tough to maintain my healthy edge. If I were to fall into my illness, it seems like it would be hard to maintain hope in this dark.

I was always most depressed in the early heat and sunshine of summer. I hated watching people all happy and healthy and I was meditating on how to kill myself. Good times—it was a case of what goes up must come down. My chemical teeter totter dipped after my winter mania.

I went to Cuba to break up the length of winter and see if this affected my illness. I went high and into psychosis. The Caribbean wind seemed to drive me on, I had to shut the doors and windows and stay inside at times. It was glorious—and frightening.

Living in a mild zone of Canada is better for me than in the volatile area of the Rocky Mountains with the Chinooks. These winds moved me with a rough treatment. I became agitated. I tried a method of breathing like snoring to counter the effects of pressure and it seemed to help.

Waterfalls and crashing surf are the opposite force ions of these winds that compress. Do you feel great to hang around moving water? Most people do. I like to hike up to a waterfall near where we live and take it all in. It is a place of beauty that soothes and inspires me to feel great, not to mention the exercise. I love to watch storms on the Pacific Ocean. Try to wipe that grin from your face with those huge waves crashing. It is another paradox of bipolar in nature: we have an uplifting force of the crash of waves and the downer of the lack of sunshine.

The whole earth flows and gives and seeks balance. If one thing is too extreme it forces change to counter it. Our own bodies rebel against us to achieve balance. Are not hurricanes, tornadoes, typhoons, monsoons, and thunder and lightening like this effect? We can learn from nature and make metaphors for bipolar. A quick release of righteous anger could be related to lightning. Use this if it helps you. Have fun with it. But please be aware of how weather may affect you. It can empower you to health. We can change our environment to better suit us. It could be as simple as moving your furniture around to get a feeling of openness to the world. Perhaps your chair will be in the sun now.

Many of our indoor spaces are not conducive to good health. The energy crisis of the early seventies slowed down our large building air exchange—it can cost a great deal of money to heat or cool exchanged air. They actually have guidelines and systems to measure the exchange rate. Have you ever walked into a store and felt the evil air? Occasionally I have to cut my time short in a building. Everything else about my life is great but faced with this air quality, I choose to vacate. The very same building at another time can have excellent air. It depends on the outside conditions and changes and how their internal system is set. I could not work for long hours in certain places, it would throw me over the edge—I get irritable and short tempered. I go outside to better air and the symptoms go away.

I find certain industrial areas tough to breathe and live in—that is one of the reasons I live where I live, the air is clean and fresh. In the dry season our air quality is going down. The rain acts like a scrubber the rest of the time. Did you know that high elevation glaciers in North America have certain chemicals that originate in Asia? We are connected in this world like our body. The earth is a living organism and we treat it like a store.

Many of us in our mania lean toward missions and wanting to save the earth. It is a great desire but please be careful. You can clean up your own life to leave a smaller footmark but be careful not to put other pursuits before your health. I would challenge you in anything you pursue: does it help you maintain balance and live toward your gift and away from your illness? If it doesn't, I would suggest backing away to gain a stronger balance. Focus on your health and perhaps later you can take it back into your life to make a difference, and not cause your health to suffer. Alone we cannot save the world but we can save ourselves and how we interact with the world. If enough of us do this, the world will be a better place.

Can you change your space to be healthier? Maybe you have too many items that distract and bring you down? Clutter can be comforting and it can be uneasy and stressing. Check out some Feng Shui. I am very affected by some of these principles. It is good to be aware. I have seen some antique Chinese furniture that uses the principles to great effect. Balance curves with the sharp edges. We dug up our front flowerbed into the shape of a wave and the whole front yard feels better. It is welcoming and in balance—before it was sharp and cold. It is amazing how our environment can affect us. What effects do you notice with the changes around you?

Are you open minded to see that the weather can affect you in complex and unusual ways? It can change depending on many factors. Have you ever lived through a threat from a weather disaster? Like a psychotic or suicidal episode your emotions need healing to recover from this—they are huge experiences that cannot be taken lightly. You have to grieve and accept and feel to heal. Living through a killing act of nature will leave you challenged: your whole view of life and its priorities and values may change. Is this not the same when facing and leaving our illness?

Bipolar is very much a storm of our minds, emotions, and bodies. Wouldn't it be nice to approach our healing in a full manner? Yes, our physical being needs treatment with bipolar. It is not just our mind—psychosis and depression can ravage our bodies. I have needed pain treatment with mental health equal to and more than times of physical harm or X-rays and surgery. Bipolar can be excruciating—much more painful than dislocations and fractures and breaks. We need to treat our whole selves. We need to heal our physical experiences of mental illness too.

Being aware of how weather can affect us is another factor that we can get on our side to know why we are feeling a certain way. There is power in self-awareness. We had big wind storms for a couple of days and it was good for me to attribute my agitation to the wind and not that I was crumbling. I noticed an increase of squealing tires in town during the wind—I was not the only one affected.

The more we can pinpoint external events having effects on our systems, the less we are judging our internal sanity and stressing ourselves to get worse. Sometimes there are simple reasons outside of ourselves why we feel a certain way. You don't have to wait for official studies to confirm this. Official studies authorize usage of products that kill thousands of people every year. Learn to trust your self-knowledge and awareness to make your own choices to feel better. You have the power to live your life in health.

Progress has even made science and commerce of weather—*The Weather Channel* was the highest watched channel in Canada last year.

Perhaps we need to return to our simple roots of weather awareness. Our very survival depended on our knowledge. Inuit people could see open water and ice reflected off the clouds. They played games in the dark winter and celebrated the changing of dark toward light. We used to sleep more in the dark winters. Now artificial lighting and commerce drives us to work around the clock.

Change of seasons can transform how we think and eat and reminisce. I find myself in the fall mourning the loss of summer, and then it becomes a strengthening time. I met a guy in the psychiatric ward who had a theory that the strengthening was connected to the rutting season in nature. How do the changes of season affect you?

It all adds up to our knowing what affects us, and to not be blown like chaff in the wind. You are in control and you can submit your control to factors knowing, and that awareness can be the key difference between feeling powerless in the lands of craze and simply smiling at the wind shredding your heart.

Points of thought and action:

#1 Does the weather have any affect on me?

#2 Does the air quality in certain buildings affect me and how? Should I avoid them?

#3 How does rain and snow and wind and storms and sun and lack of sun affect me?

#4 How do the change of seasons affect me?

#5 How does this knowledge take the pressure off of me in feeling these ways?

#6 (My personal plan.)

PERSIST THE DISCIPLINE

It would be great if we could simply install software in our head that enabled us to be disciplined and to have perseverance. And we could think of many more installations that would help us to live successfully with bipolar.

We can and do implement these changes of thinking and processing on our own with the help of books and counselors and friends and doctors. It is hard work to change our selves and our habits and our results in life—but we can and do get there.

Taking our medications as they are designed and prescribed takes discipline. You should congratulate yourself and feel great as you are able to meet your needs. We have to celebrate our achievements and merits: it will help us to repeat and grow them. Holding your head up after a hospitalization to return to work takes discipline. Look them in the eye and smile.

In my past times of mania I turned into such a disciplined monster, strangers would think I was military. My father was a soldier in WWII and his yes was yes and his no was no. I hated the tight aspects of his fatherhood but in the end it was my saving grace in psychosis. As they always did in mania and psychosis, things would get out of hand and self-discipline would reel me in. At some point my inner control would counter the crazed loon in me, and the momentum would turn toward sanity.

Just the ability to make myself stay in bed for a one hour rest would bring the healing on—the ability to make yourself think, feel, and act is sheer power. You are a reckoned force of change. You can bend in the world of change and grow deeper roots—you can adapt to the major blows in life and grow new branches. Discipline is essential for a bipolar to develop and to embrace. Bipolar itself is feeling and force without direction and control; it flows and claims you with windy tides. Discipline is our anchor that brings us back to balance.

Discipline will get you to reach for those emergency balance card approaches for depression, mania, suicide and psychosis. You will have plans of attack in place to counter these problems and you will follow your good orderly direction to balance yourself. You will walk around the block, you will talk to someone, you will take this medication, and you will call your doctor.

We need to pamper ourselves and be our own drill sergeant at the same time. And the key is to know which to focus on. You can, and have to, alternate. You absolutely have to get some exercise; you may have to be mean with yourself to get off the sofa. You may have to trick yourself into the end result. Make strong memories of how it feels after you do something hard. After exercise you feel great—plug into that and get after it, work through the bad and get to your reward.

Persistence will be tried and developed with bipolar. This thing will keep coaching us with adversity until we get through. We will be practiced athletes in the pursuit. We will be trained to compete in life and win. We that stay alive with bipolar and choose to leave our illness and live in the gift are all winners.

You will be beaten with bipolar over and over. You have to keep getting up and tweaking your approach to it: you can make it through toward completion. It will attack and you will bend and submit and counter. It will lose its power over you. It is your life and you need to build hope and persistence. Perseverance will be yours. We gain power every day we do not overdose or attempt suicide.

You have power of choice and change. Feel your power and what you have accomplished—sometimes our greatest deeds with bipolar are sitting still and keeping our mouth shut for one minute. That has been impossible for me at times, but I try to accomplish it most by channeling that manic energy and thought into movement and release. Maybe I can achieve a few seconds only—that is to be celebrated and enjoyed. Move on and live life in the gift.

Put one foot in front of the other. Get up and crawl until you can walk. Borrow someone's hope. Sit up until you can stand. Think before you do it, think and desire the outcome.

Points of thought and action:
#1   What strengthens my discipline?
#2   Why don't I want to quit fighting the illness?
#3   Why do I want to transform it into my gift?
#4   When I am challenged most, what keeps me persevering?
#5   What good have I done for myself lately that needs celebration?
#6   (My personal plan.)

SYNCHRONIZE YOUR LIFE WATCH

We want to move away from illness and into good health. We need to keep our eyes open to the changes around us. We have thought to create a new world for ourselves, but we need to develop courage to walk through the doors. We may have a tendency to stick with the old comfortable life and its easy ways, even if we hate that ill life. It is a challenge to move into a new skin and way of life.

We must use all the advantages that we can grasp. We live new lives of thought and deed. Things happen—we start down our road and the universe clicks, it falls into place. The right person walks into our life to further open the door we nudged. A school or job opens up to us. When things work together, this synchronicity is good and desired—we should welcome it into our lives and give thanks.

If we want a new life of health, we will have new events happen and meet new people. We need to embrace and accept them. You can look at everything in the world as a negative thing that conspires against you—this is an illness model of attitude. We need to look at everything that happens as preparation and training for our good and health. A warrior needs an adversary. We are bipolar warriors. Wisdom comes from struggle and observation.

It is a good thing to face life fully. If we choose joy and love and peace in spite of circumstances, we will be drawn to the good in life and opportunities will happen automatically. Focus on the good and you will be thankful when it does happen, and it will grow all around you. Embrace it with courage and humility.

Change is hard and synchronicity can be our friend to provide nudges in our new direction. I want more money to travel and an opportunity has come up that takes me out of my comfort zone. I opened the door and now I am apprehensive to walk through and take that new territory. It will be life changing and I have to ask myself if I want it. The event opportunity fits like it was designed to be, but I balk and want things to stay the way they are. I am frightened of change. It is easier to remain in the familiar negative I know.

I need money. I have not sold any books, this is my third book-length project and I can feel full time writing as my present state clearly—but the money is not here. I feel it and invite it but the reality is cloudy. I will look at this other opportunity as a great diversion; it is temporary and fits into the pursuing of the writing dream perfectly. I have to learn a whole new way of existence and interaction and job duties. The advantage is the great money and it is a temporary position that will allow me soon to be back at writing full time. I will probably be a better writer for embracing the experience.

I am scared of the unknown. It could be a great place but I'd much rather stay where I am. Perhaps this is something that we humans have ingrained in us to deal with the raw deals over the centuries: many of us have had tough lives through history and we have had to accept the demise that is life. We can lick it up in complacency.

In this century and in many parts of the world, we can make a new life for ourselves. We can design it with creativity and build it with perseverance and tenacity. Sooner or later it will fall into place. People will call you with jobs before you call them. You will run into that person on the street that you need to see. Events will happen that are smooth and designed for your situation in such a way that it is hard to deny a higher power involvement. (reference #8)

The last time I stepped up to the plate, it was reentering an old environment that I never liked. On the first day I ran into an old work friend who eased me into the whole site. I was scared and hesitant and this person just happened to be there—we laughed and reminisced and he empowered me on site. It was exactly what I needed.

We will be given what and who we need, to walk away from our illness and into our gift. Part of it is attitude—we will see the good cooperating with us for outcome. And part of it is the Law of

Attraction—what you focus on will grow and snowball and attract more of the same. (reference #3)

I need to develop friends who live their life the way they want to and not be stuck in a rut. I want to live fully and it helps me to be surrounded with people who are going for it and living large, taking big bites out of life.

The other day we took the train and a man stopped and complimented me on my hat, he said he had the same hat. I have never seen the same hat. I found his life and approach to be inspiring and interesting. He was doing what he wanted in life and making a difference for other people. We talked for fifteen minutes and he went back to his seat. I immediately felt I needed to respond to this synchronicity—I wrote my contact information and waited for a while. It still felt like I should talk to him again and my wife agreed. I walked up to his seat and we talked again for half an hour.

Because he was going to be in the town right next to mine for the next week, I offered him my number. I didn't know for certain that it was a good thing to do, but I did it—it felt right enough. It seemed like the universe was offering an opportunity and I felt like I should respond, if only for practice. I have no idea if the guy will call me but it does not matter. I had an open heart, and mind, to opportunity.

The point is for us to be open to what we ask for—do we really want it? And if we do we'd better take the synchronizations and give thanks. Embrace your graces and walk through the doors. I will walk into that opportunity and take on my new skin. I will do the job with excellence and take the money and move on. The writing money will kick in. I feel that I have much to say, I have been to places where few have been.

Psychosis has provided me with new ways of thinking and imagination. I believe the world will pay me handsomely for this. I will accept the way things happen and learn to sway with the flow. I will open my hands and watch and feel the fountain overflow. My life will surge with abundance that will spread to others.

I am now in a state of anticipation. I have three screenplays being read by producers in the U.K. and the U.S.A. I have plans to self-publish two mental health books and hit the road to speak as a bipolar coach. It has taken three years to break writing possibility through in my mind: I can feel that it is close. My new life of writing is near.

There has been much resistance to work through. I do not know anyone who makes a living at writing. I have had to form new ways of thinking a new reality and push back the walls that resist. Hundreds of people have rejected my projects and the tendency is to make me small, but I regroup and keep growing and pruning the ideas. The resistance weakens and the synchronicity clicks.

I take on courage and the assurance that all will be okay. "God grant me the serenity to accept the things I cannot change, the courage to change the things I can, and the wisdom to know the difference." –The serenity prayer of Alcoholics Anonymous.

As bipolar people we can embrace change in a real hurry and synchronicity can astound us. It can be like we make it happen—we have the power, sometimes too much power. I always struggled with becoming overwhelmed. It took practice for me to accept that things could move that fast for good. I have to continue to live my lifestyle to take the changes and fast synchronicity in stride.

I have to remind myself that I want a big life full of juice and flavor. I have to step up to the plate and swing, all the best home run hitters have been struck out swinging. Sometimes going for it they get a double on errors of the other team. Agents, Editors, and Producers have all played umpire and called me out at the plate—I swung the bat hundreds of times and missed. But I can feel the bat connect the ball and the momentum surge.

We need to be open to possibility: smile, nod, give thanks, and open your hands. Possibility is there for you to edify your life. You, too, can be a fountain overflowing to others. If we all lived the way we could and should, the world would be flowing with health and vitality.

Synchronicity is sometimes about moving toward where you should be. You will fit in and mesh and engage at the proper times. It will propel you forward in unison with your surroundings. Nice. Enjoy it and move in your gift.

Points of thought and action:

#1   What holds me back from my new life? (Don't focus on it too long.)

#2   Do I want my new life or do I choose to stay with my old life of illness?

#3 Imagine my present and future success. Am I worthy and ready to accept it?

#4 How have events and people fallen into place to assist me?

#5 I focus my thoughts, actions, and feelings on my new intended life.

#6 (My personal plan.)

LAUGH TILL THE TEARS DROP

To laugh is to heal and to gain release. Bipolar at times makes me intense and takes me to an uptight place where laughter is absent. It is a dry, terrible situation. I have to cultivate laughter.

It is great to laugh at our bipolar. It is only as epic as we allow it to be—we can laugh it down to a manageable size. We can do some terrible things with bipolar and we need to not dwell on the negative seriousness in them. We need to be easy on ourselves and one way is to laugh, to laugh at ourselves to move on in our thoughts and emotions.

When I am wound up, at times laughter is the only thing that works. It is a pressure release. It allows me to face my serious blunders and let them go. I am not always able to laugh but I do in time.

Laughter can expose our sensitivities and illuminate where we need to lighten up. Concerning stigma—perhaps you see some comedy that is badly written and uses incorrect information about bipolar. Do you still laugh if it is funny or do you get uptight about the misinformation? We are too sensitive in this world.

I have a sick sense of humor that changes. I look at it that I need as many laughs as possible to get through the tough times. I will laugh at something even if it is crude and rude. I won't repeat it but I will laugh. I need the laughs to heal and to live. If we can't laugh at something, we could loosen up. Or maybe it is telling us to write the advertisers of the program and let them know how their chosen programming is alienating their customers. We need to stand up to stigma and show the path of light. But we need to laugh.

My craziness is a subject that I have used as humor to help people to laugh. I am a healthier person for laughing at my insanity—it has helped me to let go of it. Yet there was a time when no laughing was done in my life at all, let alone on the subject of my insanity. It is in the past partially because I have laughed it there and moved on. We can use it to prioritize our life events.

The other day I was driving down a two-lane road coming to a merge section into one lane: there was a bottleneck in front of me so I kept back and watched the small car from the right lane attempting to push into the left lane; he had no signal light on and finally made it in between the two bigger vehicles. A few seconds later I saw him roll down his window and swerve in the lane and thrust his middle finger in the air at the vehicle behind him.

I was removed from the situation and my immediate reaction was to laugh at this poor man. I laughed hard and gave thanks that I was laughing. If I'd been the one who received the finger I would have had a harder time laughing but I would have tried—otherwise his act would have started a fire of anger within me. Sometimes the fire still wins over my laughter and letting go.

He could have been turning off the road. The car behind didn't even know that he wanted to lane change. No signal light, and the driver became irate. It is easy to get caught up in our own little world; everything revolves around our view. I am very hard on myself at times and I need it to be this way to live in the gift. I also need to be light and laugh at myself. I am laughing at myself right now inside for no known reason except that it feels good.

Laughter helps in our healing. I was in a hospital once that had a laughter room; I loved spending time in there with the funny audio, video, and books—it was full of ways to make you laugh. Laughing stimulates your immune system and I believe it recharges our battery and washes us clean to take on new stresses.

Have you noticed that when you are living your life out of balance and you get more and more stressed out, that you start to lose your sense of humor? I am terrible and can get into a state where I have no ability to laugh at anything. It is a gauge, a warning light of my stress level—if I can laugh I am living a good balance.

If I am too serious I need to change something. I sometimes need to remove myself from the surroundings and exercise, eat, or sleep more. The inability to laugh can inform me about my balance of living.

Do you know how to laugh? And at yourself? Do you need to build a little laughter cupboard for yourself and gather things that make you laugh? It can be part of your hope chest or plan of attack when you are ill and need balancing. You take out a file of cartoons you have cut from the paper and they lighten your situation. And if they induce no response within you, this may be a warning sign that things are worse than you thought.

You need to look after yourself. Take a day and nurture yourself, you might have to remove some stressors or change your focus, you might have to exercise and eat and not drink stimulants. Do your own balancing thing, look after yourself—watch a favorite funny movie. Pursue your plans of attack to remedy the situation before it gets too serious. Perhaps we shouldn't be in the present situation and we have to let go of it. We need to look after our best interests. Laughter is a key to maintaining our balance and staying away from the regions of illness—the manic psychosis and the suicidal depression.

Ideally, we will be hanging around people who are positive and light hearted and optimistic. We can laugh around them. We will be performing jobs and creative pursuits that keep us light and where we need to be. Periods of time will be lived when the laughter goes away but it should never go too far from your heart. If a loved one dies you may not want to laugh for a while—although in my experiences of grief I tended to laugh and cry. I find that the two are intertwined.

I remember laughter in the smoke and gathering rooms of psychiatric wards. Why were we able to laugh in our state in such a place? I believe it to be a natural coping technique we have and can develop more of. It is a pressure release that works wonders. And it can be a signpost that you are returning to sanity. How do you take yourself seriously when you are the chosen one who will save the world?

You wake up in trickles of sanity and you discover that you are surrounded by mixed levels of mentally ill people—and in your mirror is the chosen one. I found laughter to be a tool in dealing with insanity and the letting go of the seriousness. It can help you forgive and move on to leave it in the dust.

I have worked in some stressful situations that were dangerous. We found ourselves laughing out of necessity. The most gifted paramedics I have met are the twisted sense of humor ones—they laugh to survive. As bipolar people we need to laugh and not worry what others will think. Inappropriate laughter can be explained away when needed. It can also be good to be aware if someone is not capable of laughter or light heartedness, that being light around them will be a negative experience for them. In my times of depression I found myself judging the fun in others.

We have to keep our cry channels open. A little cry can reset our emotional system—at times the smallest things can trigger the release and tears. Embrace the release of tears; otherwise it will build to more negative consequences. You may find with study and practice that you can push your tear button and it is a means of coping, it will swing you back from the brink and lessen your momentum toward imbalance. It can refocus everything.

Are you aware of the last time you cried? Some of the medications we are on can steal our emotions and prevent us from truly crying or laughing. That is a tough place to be. We need to feel and respond to our emotions to be healthy and alive.

Maybe you need to build a cry file too—things that make you cry to release and feel something. In my times of psychosis I became a monster that did not feel pain or emotion. Part of my returning to sanity always involved opening my channels of feeling. Tears and laughter flooded my desert beds of emotion—it seemed to have to occur for me to get sane and real again. Once I cried and laughed again I was on my way, the second and third times were easier and the healing engaged in a quick and deep way.

In bipolar we can slip into a real deficit of emotion. We can have a backlog of events and feelings in our system. These unfelt and un-thought about situations can and do build and surge into negative consequences in our lives. We have to process the events of our lives with our minds and emotions. And the insanity can cause massive influxes of this cold confusion. How are we supposed to feel about being Jesus Christ and then telling a thousand people about it? We have to allow ourselves ways to process. It might be simply thinking about it and drawing a picture, it may be talking to a loved one and crying our heads off.

If we keep building this crap up inside of ourselves and keep adding to it, we will continue in illness. Medication can assist us in ignoring our past and our conscience and our internal strife. You are not performing a kind act to yourself by avoiding feeling emotion.

Please give yourself permission to cry and weep for the places you have been and experienced. Enough of you really did experience those crazy places to need to embrace the pain, the solitude, the confusion, and the beauty. You were there but unable to sense it fully and you have disjointed memories of it. You need to feel those places to get through them, to move on.

I have felt the greatness of my delusions of grandeur—it still motivates and fuels me. I found it scary and heady and confusing to sort through but I had to. I talked to my dead dad in a mirror—I cried and felt it then and later, and I still do. It was pivotal in my healing to this day. Insanity is an elusive friend but, in the long run from the wise viewpoint of hindsight, it can be an ally working for our good.

Part of my gift is to laugh and to cry.

Points of thought and action:
#1   Do I laugh and cry?
#2   Do I laugh and cry at bipolar?
#3   Can I give myself permission?
#4   How does it help reduce illness?
#5   Can I encourage laughter and emotion in my life?
#6   (My personal plan.)

ETHEL'S GRACE

My most gifted intervention was by Ethel. She was a farmwoman of faith. I had been flying high and my truck was stuck in the snow and my wings were clipped. I was to do great things and I could not get to town. Frozen water crystals stopped me and I sought her house.

She cared for my mind. She did simple things like warm my feet and feed my soul. She played spiritual music that spoke to me. She covered me in a blanket. She gave me warm drink. These are important things in healing. We sometimes lose touch with the basic things in life searching for the perfect drug and solution. One cure will do it. Maybe we are missing many of the little things like warm feet and drink and company.

Perhaps we need to live in community and take care of each other. To keep each other fed and warm and nurtured. This can be part of our solution, a gift of interdependence.

How do you need to be treated in your times of need? Do you need to treat yourself to a hotel room from time to time and maybe even a holiday? Do you work yourself into the hospital? Could you pamper yourself and lower your stimuli and take your medication and talk to your doctor? Perhaps these methods could prevent a hospitalization.

Make up care packages for your tough times. If you are still in your hospitalization phase, a care package of goodies can ease you in. This should include self-coaching audio to limit the negative effects of your stay, and to maximize the positive.

Remember that when we can prevent our extremes we reduce our body's chemical reaction to the illness. Reduce your highs and you most likely will reduce your reactive state of depression. Physics applied to mental health—reduce your energy and limit the effects of the same energy. We add friction and brake force to slow down. In depression, you may need to increase your energy and channel your focus: medication, fast music, even caffeine to get you exercising to prevent that chemical droop into depression. The longer you allow yourself to be in a low or a high, the harder it can be to escape.

We need to learn to prevent and reduce the severity and length of our episodes. Then our bipolar is not as deep a chemical effect in our systems—we do not get thrown around as much or for as long. I have researched these theories with my life. Do they work for you? Adjust them and make your own. This is your life.

Give yourself some of Ethel's grace to look after your basic needs—perhaps you can slow the chemical effects down; someday you will stop the illness in its tracks. You will be left with the gift called You.

Points of thought and action:
#1 What is the care I need in my various states?
#2 How can I ensure that I receive it?
#3 Can I coach my network to treat me differently in my rough times?
#4 Can I make myself a care package?
#5 What do I need right now to achieve health and balance?
#6 (My personal plan.)

WRAP THE GIFT AND TEAR IT OPEN

You are the designer of your preferred way of living. You must take your focus off of your illness and the negatives in your life. The more you look at it the more it will increase to take control. Lift up your eyes onto your desired life. Focus on your good and great future.

It is your stage play and you get to design and decorate the set and dress the actors. It is your story; enjoy writing, casting, directing, and living it. Focus on the results you want: see, feel, and taste where you want to be. Wrap your empowered thinking and words in that direction.

Don't let the cold people drag you down. You are a new person going for your new life: you can act independent of what others think. All of my great steps to leave the illness and live in the gift had others waiting and willing to comment and direct me that I was doing something wrong. I chose not to hear their negative, but still took their counsel.

Do you hear what you need to do to be healthier? Are you in touch with your intuition? Can you learn to trust and separate it from the attacks of mistaken thinking of illness? We are living a challenge with rewards waiting. What are your rewards for living in health?

How are your self-talk recordings playing out for you?

Are my approaches too alternative? Do I not give the doctor enough power? My doctor is one of my tools. I use my doctor and medications to climb out of this dark hole in space. I do not submit my life to those two methods alone. Anything can help us. What helps you?

Electroshock Therapy can save your life when nothing else will. It can also cause you harm. I want to work hard to avoid those suicidal islands because I don't want Electroshock. And, once again, please hear that Electroshock can save your life and any memory impairment can be temporary. Doesn't it make sense to prevent the severity of our moods by living our lives the way they were intended? Yes, bipolar stands in the way of our lives. Anything can be an excuse or a solution—change your way of seeing things and you will modify their reality and their effect on your existence. (reference # 8)

The masses are driven like buffalo over the cliff. We cannot choose the mass way of approaching illness. Focusing on the bad will bring more bad. Medicalization and measurement and management will grant persistence to the problem. Intend your new life and take actions toward it. You will attract what you intend and think on. (reference #3)

Be flexible and able to mute your judgments to choose your intended reaction to every event. You have the power to live with intention. Step toward it now—your gifts are hidden within and around you. They have waited your entire life: with time they can even be harder to see. If your eye only sees illness and negativity, you will lose vision. Take your eyes off the bad in your life and replace it with good: think, feel, desire, and take steps toward it in reality. You will dream, feel, think, and live. I cannot do it for you. Your dreams are yours to live and share.

Kick out the reasons you want to hold onto illness. Move toward your promised land. Love yourself and others. Lift yourself above what the world would have for you.

We have choices in life to grow our intent into fruition. I have wanted to be a writer for years and put it off. I always had to do something else first. I now have this non-fiction, one memoir, one novel, one novella, seven screenplays, poetry, and short stories. I have yet to find an agent or publisher, yet I am developing my craft. I do not want to be a flash in the pan writer. It would have been great to sell the first book immediately. But in the long run this works better because it has developed the tenacity and skills to write. Writers write and that is what I do. I write. I never used to do this. I desired it for a long time and it grew in intent and purpose. I thought and studied about writers and shaped my ways to follow in their steps.

It is part of my gift. I can let go and follow the inspired route. I can trust the creative force with the quality and concentrate on the quantity. This is great. The seeds of dream grew in my mind and sprouted in thoughts, action and desire. These thoughts and actions became habits and are becoming a way of life.

I now look at the whole world differently. I can manage it if I can write stories. I can deal with stress and put positive spin on anything that happens—now it is all material and experience to lean on for novel flavor. Not that I am avoiding reality and dealing with the world. But, yes, I absolutely cannot swallow all that the media serves up. I can't deal with the full details of the murders and disasters. I could live back a few hundred years with the capacity to only know about my immediate surroundings. What truly matters is where I am and to focus on the whole world is detrimental to my emotional health.

I always found the world to be upsetting and hard to digest. Everyone has different values and priorities. I also believe in the evil and good in the world. Have you seen examples of both? I have heard two non-spiritual people who lived in Africa talk about how attuned to spirituality they became. It was vivid and hung thick in the air and conspired for their demise. They had to become more spiritual to counter the evil workings of spirit. When they lived in North America they had no inkling of spirituality.

Our religion major is becoming more and more greed, shareholder profit and consuming. We focus on this created need and it is all we see. Please don't get me wrong, I was shopping yesterday and loved it. But life is much more powerful and joyful when I am not connected to fulfilling my wants to the exclusion of my needs. I need to interact with people more than buying electronics. I need to live in balanced bipolar more than buying a bigger house and vehicle.

We are spiritual beings; it is all around, about, and within us. Whether you are tuned in or tuned out is who you are. It can change—my spiritual life has changed many times and will continue to. I believe in love; I see it in nature, the sacrifice to sustain and continue life. Love is good and love of self repels and excludes illness. If we learn to listen to our needs and be true to our values and priorities, we will tend not to be ill. If you love your body and whole self, is your personality less concerned with your habits of behavior and thought?

Can you change your personality? Yes I believe you can and you must, as an experienced bipolar. It will change your personality for you and will challenge you with many more changes. We need to create the power in your thoughts and actions to counter these waves of mood. You can learn to listen to your spirit—your intuition will show you the way. We are responsible for our actions and life.

It is you who chooses how to act and react—you are your personality. It sounds scary and creepy to change your personality but is that not what many of us need? A step at a time.

I have trouble letting go of rage and anger at times but it is I who lose, most every time. I can get that good purposeful anger going and it can focus my actions and words to challenge and make change—this is great. And then there are times when I am on a tangent that does no one any good, especially me. I am improving and am able to choose to let go: I am not perfect, but on a journey called life.

Well this is the end. Do you feel the flash of possibility? You develop how you take these next pictures in your life. You make your choices of thought and action. Have I upset you? I don't want you to agree with my ways; I want you to know and live your ways. If you've made it this far you are on board. This is big. This is your life to live or die. This is the ultimate you that lives your life instead of watching others. Your choice is to smile in the midst of struggle.

I make progress and choose joy in spite of the circumstances. I give myself plenty of challenge and rewards to move onward to my desired life. I can do anything I want to.

I can write for a living. Hey, I wrote this book and I'm coaching on bipolar—it is fun to interact. I will help many people out and this will help me. I am not about material things first, I want to live a higher purpose and bipolar showed me new vistas of possibility and creation. I want to give back and be in balance.

I have pursued honesty in this writing and I hope that it has shone through to your heart to inspire you to be honest. That is where it all starts—we need to get over and through our self-deceptions. Prepare your ground for the seeds of possibility with brutal honesty. Allow yourself to dream again, this is your natural fertilizer. Do you remember how to dream? It may take practice. Dream in the daytime and play your life to fruition.

Accept reality as the way people need to live. Love them and do not judge. Accept yourself and forgive your bipolar ways. There are seeds of greatness in the ashes of your bipolar beast. Burn and offer it up to collect the dividends. Be careful, your bipolar creature can turn on you, be wary at all times. Someone, in mistaken thinking could read this about burning and feel the need to burn something in reality.

Like they say in A.A. "Take what you need, and leave the rest." Take the best. This is your springboard to develop and write your own guidebook. You have unique solutions to your problems. May this book act like your gatekeeper; you can be off the map and need a guide to bridge realities. I am here to tell you that you are not the only one to experience those horrible thoughts and actions.

It is okay to flounder and try new things; strange pursuits can assist us toward health. Do not judge but discover the things that you need to do. You have been to some strange lands as a bipolar and it makes sense that you may be driven to perform in some strange ways to deal with those realities. Perhaps unique art and solutions may come out of it.

I believe we bipolar people have been chosen; if we look at it this way, everything falls into place—we are given the opportunity for greatness in our life pursuit. It is the ultimate training ground and facility. I have made it through bipolar and take these skill sets with me. I am unstoppable in the pursuit of my dream. This life is what I make it. I turn my eyes to focus on where I need to be, and take steps toward it. I am there now. I smile and take another step.

What will you leave as a legacy? Reflect more and take risks. You will be a happy wrinkled old person.

ADVANTAGES OF BIPOLAR

There are many famous people who have bipolar. They have contributed to society in amazing ways. For most, bipolar assisted them in their contributions. We share many of the same challenges that bipolar gave their lives. We also possess the opportunity to share many of their same bipolar gifts.

I mention this to give you hope that you can make it to wherever you need to be in your life. You will come across the lists of famous people in your research. Remember that it is not necessarily a good thing to be on a famous list. It depends how you look at it. But be encouraged.

We also share many of the following bipolar gift sides: Can you see your potential in these? Make yourself notes of how, why, and where you could go with these. Can you also identify potential problems?

Example: Focus

"Good concentration, can stick with a problem to find the solution, intense, problem solver, inventor—the lack of focus could make a great worker with children's attention spans. I have to be aware of others when I focus. I need to let my partner know that this hour is my time to be creative—please do not interrupt me."

Stretch your thinking with possibility and angles of approach. By no means is this list complete. Please make your personal one.

Active mind
Belief
Changeable
Communicative

Compassion
Concentration
Connection with our muse
Creative
Depression
Desire
Discipline
Empathy
Energy
Experience
Extrovert
Feeling
Focus
Go with the flow
Grandiose thoughts
Highly sexed
Honesty
Humility
Innovative solutions
Imagination
Intensity
Internal journeys
Introvert
Joyful in spite of circumstances
Long suffering
Mania
Mixed States
Movement
New ideas
Observant
Pain
Psychosis
Questioning
Realism
Sense of humor
Social courage
Trusting in the journey
Understanding

Unlimited
Varied
Wisdom
Zaniness

The same famous bipolar people share traits with famous non-bipolar people: tenacity, belief, patience, drive, hunger, dreaming, and risk taking. But does not bipolar offer us the opportunity to progress in all of these traits too?

—To live dreams and die full of ripeness.

REFERENCES

#1 Beyond Crazy: Journeys Through Mental Illness
   Julia Nunes & Scott Simmie
   McClelland & Stewart Ltd. 2002

#2 Night Falls Fast: Understanding Suicide—Alfred A. Knopf
   Publisher 1999
   Touched with Fire—Manic Depressive Illness and the Artistic
   Temperament (I used her general ideas of bipolar advantage for
   creativity)
   Simon and Schuster Publisher 1993—Both written by Kay
   Redfield Jamison, Ph.D.

#3 The Law of Attraction
   Hicks family in Texas
   Box 690070
   San Antonio, Texas 78269

#4 Think and Grow Rich
   Napoleon Hill
   Random House Publishing Group 1976

#5 Excuse Me, Your Life is Waiting: The Astonishing Power of
   Feelings
   Lynn Grabhorn
   Hampton Roads Publishing Company, Inc. 2000

#6 Millionaire Next Door: The Surprising Secrets of America's
   Wealthy

Thomas J Stanley, Dr. / William D. Danko, Ph.D.
Longstreet Press 1996

#7 The Wealthy Barber
David Chilton
Three Rivers Press 1997

#8 The Power of Intention
Wayne W. Dyer, Dr.
Hay House, Inc. 2004

#9 Secrets of the Millionaire Mind
T. Harv Eker
Collins 2005

Alcoholics and Narcotics Anonymous
Twelve step principles.
Hazleden

RECOMMENDED VIDEOS TO STRETCH OUR THINKING:

The Secret

What the Bleep Do We Know: How Far Down the Rabbit Hole Do You Want To Go?

Check out the website for this book: www.thebipolarguide.com

NON-SUICIDE CONTRACT

Initial & Date

_____ I, _____(Name), born _____(Birthdate) will die of natural causes, accident or disease, on a date unknown to me.

_____ I choose not to take my own life.

_____ When I have suicidal thinking, I will call _____ _____&_____.

_____ When I have suicidal thinking, I will call the Crises Line @ _____(#).

_____ I will not perform suicidal actions.

_____ I will _____ _____, which helps me to feel and think better.

_____ I will learn to change my suicidal thoughts. I will learn to control my thoughts.

_____ I will talk to my health care professionals: _____ _____&_____.

_____ I will take medicine that soothes my ravaged mind and leans me toward balance.

_____ I will learn to recognize what triggers my slide into a depressive and suicidal state.

_____ I will strive to not do the things that cause my chemistry to dip toward depression.

_____ I will become an expert on suicide and suicidal thinking to empower myself to choose life.

_____ I will study this Bipolar Guide to the Gift book and apply its principles and develop my own approaches to reduce bipolar illness, change my perspective, and develop bipolar advantages.

_____ I will take control of my thoughts, actions, and feelings.

_____ I will work with my health care professionals to discover medications and remedies that help.

_____ I will always reach out to other human beings or animals for unconditional love and acceptance.

_____ I will share this contract with someone and agree to live to my best ability.

_____ I choose not to engage in self-pity.

_____ If my above mentioned allies are uncooperative or they themselves die, I will network and rewrite this contract with new allies.

_____ I choose to help others with my life. I keep my eyes open to my true purpose.

_____ (N a m e)

_____(S i g n a t u r e)

_____(Date)

_____ (W i t n e s s)

_____(S i g n a t u r e)

_____(Date)